How to
BARTER for
PARADISE

How to
BARTER for
PARADISE

My Journey Through 14 Countries,
Trading Up from an Apple to a House in Hawaii

Michael Wigge

Translated by Tobi Haberstroh

Skyhorse Publishing

www.skyhorsepublishing.com

10 9 8 7 6 5 4 3 2 1

Library of Congress Cataloging-in-Publication Data is available on file.

ISBN: 978-1-62636-417-2

Printed in the United States of America

CONTENTS

HAWAII, HERE I COME!

Mars, Pluto, and Jupiter were my constant companions when I was a child and nothing fascinated me more than the universe. I still remember how one Christmas I asked for every book that had anything to do with the realm of the stars. Of course, I also asked for the newest toy space station with a moon unit and extra intergalactic telescope. One year later I got a real telescope. Its 32X magnification, additional finder scope, and various sunlight filters infinitely increased my desire to be near the stars. But before the Easter Bunny even came in the spring, my telescope had disappeared from the living room cabinet. My fear of the neighbor, whom I observed with my telescope and who had made it clear with his emphatic waving that he would rather watch his evening TV show alone, created knots in the pit of my stomach.

So, for better or worse, I focused on the things that our own planet had to offer. I devoted myself to the far-flung regions of the earth—initially with my student atlas. The most far-flung region that I could find was, without a doubt, the group of islands known as Hawaii. That moment, I declared Hawaii as my dream destination. White beaches kissed by low-hanging palms, tropical mountain peaks, water as clear as glass . . . During puberty, the fantasy of flower-bedecked, dancing Hawaiian girls added itself to this enticing list. So what was more fitting than the thought of owning my own home there? A Hawaiian dream house!

From then on, the front of my wardrobe was decorated with a poster of Hawaii, which I unfortunately had to cut in half to continue opening the doors. The sides of it were gradually decorated with Hawaiian postcards, maps of the islands, and of course, the state license plate with the famous rainbow.

The Hawaiian dream house unfortunately remained a dream as I started my career; however, I was able to live out my wanderlust.

I didn't just gaze at my student atlas—I traveled to seventy countries and made my passion into a career by writing about my travels. I was a curious visitor to the Yanomami Indians in the Amazon who laughed at me for managing to miss shooting an anteater that was so close by. I was able to visit bizarre capsule hotels in Tokyo and I went up against Sumo wrestlers. At the Spanish Tomatina Festival, I wore white and had tomatoes thrown at me. I traveled to Antarctica on an expedition ship, and Queen Elizabeth gave me a stern look when I showed up to her fiftieth Jubilee at Buckingham Palace dressed as Prince Henry VIII (no joke).

But none of that ever got me a house in Hawaii. What to do? Should I travel to Hawaii and appear on a millionaire bachelorette show? Or would a headline appear in a tabloid one day proclaiming, "German Travel Writer Behind Bars after Attempting to Squat in a House in Hawaii!" Unlikely!

I remembered that on my last trip through North America I had met a young Canadian who successfully bartered up from a paper clip to a house within a year on an online bartering website. A paperclip as the down payment on a house—not bad, I thought! Even if the house wasn't in sunny Hawaii.

Unfortunately, I'm not very good at closing deals online (I've still never won an auction on eBay), and also unfortunately, I didn't have a year to spend on the project. Nevertheless, the idea fascinated me. Why couldn't I do what I had been doing for years—travelling the world—except this time, I would barter. I would give myself six months to travel the world and barter, barter, barter. In this way I could learn an unbelievable amount about trading and the value of goods in different cultures—fascinating! And totally coincidentally, I would get closer and closer to my dream. At the end, I could unlock the door to my Hawaiian dream house. Sounds simple enough, right?

It wasn't simple at all. But I was lucky: my reputation as a man of extravagant travels preceded me. The German TV station ZDFneo offered to finance my bartering world tour along with two cameramen,

Jakob and Dominik. The deal was that I had to make my bartered-for house in Hawaii available to anyone—the viewers and readers—who wanted to vacation there and could offer a trade for it. I would have two hundred days and I had to set foot on all six continents to learn about and report on the culture of barter on each of them. I accepted the offer enthusiastically. Soon, I would be moving into my house in Hawaii as a bartering expert!

Standing in her apartment doorway, my neighbor burst into laughter when I told her about my plan. She said I could leave the key to my apartment with her if I decided I never wanted to come back from Hawaii. I watched her walk down the stairs and heard her murmur as she shook her head: "A house in Hawaii . . . what nonsense. . . . No wonder the natives and the Queen thought he was ridiculous!"

Maybe she was right. But twenty-five years had gone by since I hung that poster of Hawaii on my wardrobe. The way I saw it, it was time to get down to it and make this dream a reality. I believe everyone should try to fulfill their dreams sometime in their lives. Who doesn't have one of those constant dreams that accompanies them through life? And there's always that voice in your head saying that it isn't a good idea, isn't appropriate, isn't realistic, and that you couldn't do it anyway.

But this voice might be wrong. And so, after a twenty-five-year delay, I was off.

BITTEN BY THE BUG

Germany

I'm standing at a little fruit stand in Mainz, attempting to buy an apple—my first object to barter with. It needs to be a pretty, healthy, delicious apple—an organic one. In Berlin organic is trendy.

I proudly explain my project to the salesman. I tell him that this very apple is my startup capital for a Hawaiian dream house, and that I'm well on the path to fulfilling a childhood dream via persistent bartering. But before I can trade my seventy-nine cents for the organic apple, the salesman's mood darkens. These young people with their crazy ideas. Always more, always farther away, always knowing better. They're never happy with what they have. Can anyone these days still enjoy the simple things?

I stare back at him. I had never expected this kind of reaction.

I take my apple but the uneasy feeling remains. I begin to have my first doubts about the real appeal of this sort of transaction. How would people in Asia, Africa, and America react to me attempting to trade for my own benefit? Not like this fruit seller, I hoped.

I approach my first potential trade partner, a middle-aged tourist from Konstanz, and I forget my rocky start. Without a long explanation I offer him the now bitten apple (you should always be sure of the quality of your offering) for a spontaneous barter. The tourist laughs and offers me an already opened pack of cigarettes. We shake hands very officially to seal the deal. When he leaves, I watch him from a distance for a while and see how he happily bites into the apple.

I'm pleased that I don't have to take the reaction of the fruit seller as a bad omen. I've already increased the value of my first object after one trade. And the fact that my bartering partner received something healthy in exchange for something unhealthy is a pleasant thought. So now I have sixteen cigarettes in my hand, which I can only offer to a smoker, obviously. After a while I seem to have fewer and fewer cigarettes. Soon, I run into a mother who is walking with her daughter. I make sure that the daughter is old enough; after all, we're talking about cigarettes here.

But unfortunately, the two women pass up the offer. They just quit smoking, the daughter explains, but I'm not ready to give up so easily:

Me: "These cigarettes are particularly good."

Mother: "No thank you, we don't need them."

Daughter: "No, we quit."

Me: "One little drag after dinner can't hurt . . ."

Mother: "Oh yes it can."

After that very clear statement, I find myself standing alone again with my cigarettes in the town square. A husband and wife walk up to me with sad smiles, as if they pity the poor guy selling cigarettes even though it's impossible to lure people in that way these days. I explain to them that I am trying to move into my Hawaiian dream house in two hundred days. The man rushes past me and gestures wildly to his wife that she shouldn't get involved with crazy guys on the street. However, the wife senses the chance for a little promo of her own. She is an author, and pulls out her freshly printed book on Saarland, a village in Germany, from her purse. I leaf through it and among photos of landscapes and darling villages a chapter title catches my eye: "SUCCESS!" is printed in fat letters at the top of the page. Yes, Saarland is known to produce successful people—ever since Oskar Lafontaine's (from Saarland) political career took off, no one can deny it. Maybe I should take this word as a positive sign for my mission. The author signs the book for me, takes the cigarettes, and follows her disapproving husband.

I start reading up on Saarland so that I have some good arguments for my third barter: Saarland has the same population as Cologne, has six highways, and you can get culinary delicacies there such as Dibbelabbes or dandelion salad. Will that persuade someone?

A saleswoman in the town square is interested in my offering because she is so taken by my knowledge of Dibbelabbes. She retrieves a kitschy rabbit statue made of silver metal from her shopping bag. She was going to give it to an employee as a gift, but I convince her that the book with the Dibbelabbes recipe would bring her a lot more enjoyment. She agrees but for inexplicable reasons does not want to part with the bed of moss on which the little rabbit sits. We argue back and forth until she finally gives it up, mostly because she is in a rush.

Now the silver bunny sits on the dashboard of my van, wrapped in nice paper and traveling toward Siegburg in North Rhine-Westphalia. On the way there, I try my luck at a rest stop off the highway, but it is apparently the wrong place to offer up a kitschy silver rabbit. The first driver I speak to refuses to talk to me at all, and he seems almost scared as he makes his escape. Another truck driver gestures as though swatting away an annoying fly when I try to give him the rabbit through his window. He's also in a rush to get going.

But there is a young couple vacuuming their car who remind me of Marc Terenzi and Sarah Connor (before their divorce of course), and they seem a bit more open-minded. They let me look in their trunk. It's full of junk—it looks as if they've just been waiting here for someone to offer to barter with them. Aside from various sprays, a hand broom, and lots of newspapers, there is a first aid kit, expired but unused. The young man, alias Marc Terenzi, agrees to the barter. I ask him and his girlfriend whether they have any doubts about continuing on their way without a first aid kit. Sarah Connor's doppelganger replies that the lucky rabbit would help her a lot more in an emergency than that old box. I see things differently, so I am happy to trade for the kit. I drive on with it to my next destination, Siegburg.

In this little city with its historic center there is a 125-year-old prison, which is now home to a juvenile detention center. I was able to convince the warden to let me stop by before I began my trip. After all, a prison is a place where no one has their own money; what makes more sense than bartering? I was also curious how exchanges between prisoners and officers took place. Were there friendships? Hostilities?

Images pop up spontaneously in my brain of prisoners trading for forbidden items like drugs and tools for escaping, smuggled in by friends and relatives. Is there anything to these fantasies?

The prison greets me with high brick walls and barbed wire. When I approach the entry gate and see how they inspect visitors, I feel like I'm in a scene from a movie. The cliché of nail files baked into cakes runs through my head again, and I can't help but think of the first aid kit, which surely contains a pair of scissors. Was my last exchange not as clever as I thought? Would I cause difficulties for myself and the prisoners? I approach the gate with a guilty conscience. I give the guard my ID and show security the kit with a grin. When I say "This is my trade object," the guard looks at me with some surprise through his bulletproof glass, but then waves me through with a frown. Now I'm inside the jail with my first aid kit complete with scissors. I still have the feeling I'm doing something forbidden.

I'm glad to finally meet the security guard who had agreed to speak with me on the topic of "bartering in prison." We walk down a hall of the correctional facility that is broken up by many barred doors. The security guard tells me that bartering is commonplace for the prisoners. It is the only way for them to get many coveted items that they can't simply buy. The administration tolerates it so long as the bartered items don't exceed a certain value, but they firmly quash bartering for illegal items such as drugs or more expensive items like electronic devices.

Later, I meet several imprisoned youths, almost all of whom are there for violent crimes. Serkan, who was sentenced to two years in juvenile detention, invites me into his cell. It is about eighty square feet but feels like forty, and contains a bed, a toilet, and a TV. A little piece of the sky can be seen through a small barred window. Serkan tells me that being in prison is obviously not easy, but certain conveniences like the TV, working as a mechanic, and friendly swapping with other prisoners make the whole thing a bit easier. He explains how his cell neighbor, David, has become his best friend. Since the cell doors are open daily from 3:30 to 8:30 in the evening, they can hang out. Serkan introduces me to Frank. He is about twenty and also imprisoned for a violent offense. Frank shows me the joinery where he works every day and talks about how hard the first weeks in prison were and how his girlfriend left him. But he also says that a good relationship with the officers in the correctional facility helped him get through the hardest part of his time in prison. I'm surprised to hear that the interaction between the guards and the prisoners is so trusting. I ask whether there is also a lot of distrust and fear, but Frank stands by his statement and tells me about long conversations, patient listening, encouragement, and many offers of help. I'm impressed, but I do look over to the two guards who are standing in the room with crossed arms, nodding happily. Is Frank just trying to win brownie points with them? I would have been happier to have this conversation without chaperones.

I take a little walk across the yard with Serkan and Frank. I feel a little uneasy knowing that I don't belong to this world where the prisoners cope with their difficult reality every day. But Frank and Serkan seem to trust me. They tell me more about their everyday lives. They talk about the anti-violence therapy that they have attended in prison. They explain that they aren't as easy to provoke anymore, which they prove on our walk through the yard as other prisoners shout, "Hey, jerk-offs, what's that gay shit you're spouting?" Serkan and Frank's composure is admirable.

On the other end of the yard I see lots of prisoners conversing through the barred windows of their cells even though they are out of each other's sight. Their calls echo off the yard walls so that I can only hear little bits of conversation: "Dude!" "... Matze says ..." "Oh sh** ..." The yard is like a sea of voices with big waves breaking against the walls. I call to two prisoners in their windows to ask if they can really have a conversation with each other like that. A voice answers: "Well, it's better than staring at the wall." It seems that in these circumstances the exchange of words is more important than the exchange of objects. Back in the cell block, I offer Serkan and Frank my first aid kit (with scissors) under the attentive and somewhat nervous watch of a security guard. Serkan and Frank look at the guard for a nod of approval. The kit is unopened in Frank's hands. What happens if they find the scissors? A weapon for an imprisoned criminal . . . provided by me. . . . It seems to take an eternity for Serkan to open the box, and the whole time I am wondering how I could be so stupid as to bring an object like this to trade in a prison. It seems to me like the guard is uneasy too; he watches us unwaveringly.

What happens then is nothing like a movie. No one tries to hide the scissors under his shirt; no security guard throws himself at us to wrestle the dangerous object away. Serkan and Frank look at the guard questioningly and at me somewhat reproachfully. The guard gives me a what-is-this-crap look like an annoyed dad who just caught his son breaking the rules. I fall right into that role, shrugging my shoulders casually as if to say I don't have any idea how this could have happened. Luckily, Frank and Serkan salvage the situation by courteously turning down the barter and then explaining the prison rules to me.

Ten minutes later I am standing before the warden of the correctional facility, still feeling a bit like a naughty little boy. But the scissors incident is prudently not discussed further. Instead, the wryly smiling warden offers me a wooden box with an ornate lid made by a prisoner. Inside is a bottle of sherry from his private stores. I don't have to debate for long—with a hearty handshake, the bottle of sherry changes hands. The deal is done, and the first aid kit with scissors disappears without fanfare into the warden's desk.

The Nuclear Barter

I drive on to Cologne with the sherry bottle in its wooden box. I have a friend there who works in the so-called bartering business. Simon explains that the company he works for sells TV ad minutes and print ad space to companies and sometimes accepts the company's product as payment instead of money. For example, he tells me, at the moment there are ninety thousand bottles of smoothies in their warehouse. It's Simon's job to then sell the bartered items for as much profit as possible. Simon's clients love to use this payment option since it allows them to pay even if they have a small advertising budget. So it can happen that a car company pays Simon for an ad with seventeen compact cars. It all started when artisans and tradesmen began to barter their wares instead of paying with money due to money shortages during wartime. After the war, a small professional bartering scene arose, in which there are currently four active companies. Simon tells me that because of his job, he has become a real professional in niche markets. He can see potential buyers that haven't even crossed the manufacturers' minds.

I would have loved to discuss this interesting topic for longer, but, after all, I'm on a mission. I want to trade a bottle of sherry for something of higher value—not an easy job when I'm up against a bartering pro like Simon. So I offer him the sherry in its wooden box while explaining its unique value: the box was made by prisoners. Unmoved, Simon gazes at the Cologne Cathedral through the large glass windows of his office. As an experienced bartering pro, he is not very impressed by the rarity of an item. He is much more concerned with the material worth of the item. He is interested only in the bottle of sherry. He disappears into the warehouse and reappears with thirty-two of the ninety thousand smoothies. I'm dissatisfied with this offer, so I emphasize the high quality of the sherry. And I am successful: Simon returns to the warehouse and offers an additional twenty-eight smoothies, making it clear that that is his final offer. We seal the deal with a handshake, as one should.

A few minutes later a dramatic scene is playing out in front of Simon's office. I hopelessly attempt to balance fifty smoothie bottles in my arms, using my chin to give the pile the necessary stability. One smoothie falls, then a few more, and finally I'm standing there with empty hands, watching the bottles roll around on the ground. I repeat the same performance once more as I try to get the smoothies into my van.

I simply haven't given enough forethought to the logistics of transporting large or unwieldy items. To add insult to injury, I see Simon ride by on his bike as I collect all the bottles from the ground yet again. He grins and waves, holding the bottle of sherry in his hand. A true bartering pro, he could see right to the true advantages of the item. I clearly still have a lot to learn on this trip.

The passersby continue on silently when I ask them to free me from at least one of the fifty annoying smoothie bottles by bartering with me. An older woman just asks me, "Boy, what've ya got rollin' around on the ground there?" before turning the corner with her walker.

As I continue my hopeless attempt to reach my van, I realize that on top of everything, I am right in the path of an anti-nuclear power march. But before I'm steamrolled by the chanting crowd carrying banners for wind and solar energy, I have an idea that could save me. I quickly join in on the demonstrators' chants: "Stop nuclear power! Stop nuclear power! Shut it down! Shut it down!" I inconspicuously mix in some advertising for my smoothies, without departing from the anti-nuclear theme: "Soft drinks, not atom-cocktails! Enjoy while you shut it down! Smooooothies! Delicious Smooooothies!" I definitely attract attention, but it's all uncomfortable, irritated looks.

So instead, I go down to a stand set up by the Social Democratic Party on the edge of the action. The red smoothies could definitely be a great advertisement, or maybe the comrades are just thirsty. Barter seems to me like a truly social democratic endeavor. I approach the person in charge of the balloons and offer him my smoothies for the helium gas tank he is using to fill them. He waves me off, and when I don't relent he snaps, "I said no!"

I move on to the Green Party, which is demonstrating for the abandonment of nuclear power. At their stand, they have those familiar yellow barrels with the radioactive symbol on the side, used for disposing of radioactive waste. I talk to the leader about my Hawaiian dream. He asks what that has to do with nuclear power. I realize that I haven't given that any thought and I start to lose control of the situation. However, pragmatism wins out at the stand, and the leader consults with the party base, which seems excited by the prospect of refreshment. The leader agrees to the barter, but he also wants me to make a little statement of support for the Green Party. Nothing to it, I think, and I say confidently to my video camera: "The Green Party is for stopping nuclear power, so vote Green!"

I leave the stand free of fifty smoothies but with a medium size waste barrel. I schlep it back to the van on my shoulders. Balancing it and walking through the city is not exactly child's play, but I manage to walk for a few minutes at a time. Compared to the smoothies, which I had to collect off the ground regularly, it's a blessing. And the barrel has another unexpected benefit: it raises my activist status considerably. People going by in cars give me a thumbs-up, and passersby shout out statements of support: "Yeah! Down with nuclear power!" At first, I feel like I have to try to explain the situation, but then I start to enjoy the role. After all, it wasn't easy to get this barrel. So I grin back, proud to have contributed to the demonstration in my own way.

Herman Forever

I drive toward Paderborn in Westphalia to visit Frank, an acquaintance who restores old bathtubs in a barn. Before I started my trip, Frank assured me that I could barter for one of his bathtubs, as long as the item up for trade was of comparable value. When he sees the waste barrel, his face gets serious. He tries to remain polite as he explains that he doesn't have much need for a barrel like that.

Luckily, I'm ready for this reaction. I've prepared a list of suggestions for alternative uses for the barrel, which I present to him immediately:

Waste barrel as bar stool

Waste barrel as drum

Waste barrel as hiding spot

Waste barrel as bodybuilding weight

Waste barrel as full body massage roller

Frank laughs and allows himself to be convinced by my unconventional suggestions and my Oscar-worthy performance.

He takes me into his barn and presents a choice of objects to trade: an old bicycle with a flag, an even older sewing machine, and a broken red riding lawn mower no younger than the other things. The decision is easy. Having a riding mower is another one of my childhood dreams that I now unexpectedly have the chance to fulfill.

We change the mower's friction wheel together so that an hour later it actually starts up with a loud rattle. Frank notices the glint in my eye at the sight of the working machine, so he puts forth another condition for the barter: before I can take my treasure with me, I have to mow the field behind his barn. It's over three and a half acres—approximate mowing time: at least five hours. I want to start right away. Frank takes visible delight in standing on the waste disposal barrel watching as I mow endless stripes in the field. As I disappear farther into the distance, he occasionally waves encouragingly. After a half hour he seems to take pity on me and waves me in. I finally get the handshake I've been waiting for to make the barter official.

The next leg of my journey is Lake Constance. I've made a date with a bartering circle there in the small town of Wangen. They have been practicing bartering as an alternative to money for many years. But first I have to get there with my new acquisition, and perhaps along the way there will be some opportunity or another for a little business transaction.

I let the mower ride around a few nice areas on the long trip across Germany, rattling over roads and fields. Over time, my affection for the little guy has grown so much that I lovingly christen him Herman.

I notice some surprised locals waving at us from the distance on the way down a steep slope to the Lorelei on the Rhine. I never find out whether they are excited at the sight of Herman or annoyed by the noise and exhaust. In St. Goar I drive the thirsty, loudly droning Herman into a gas station. I fill up the wonderful tractor with five gears (including reverse!) under the perplexed gaze of the station attendant. A short while later the news of my presence seems to have spread.

The sexton of the nearby church comes to ask me just what I'm doing by riding a lawn mower through town. I tell him what's on my mind and that Herman is just a stop on the way to a house in Hawaii. The sexton doesn't seem to understand such worldly affairs; he just grabs his camera to snap some photos to have proof of this strange event.

A little later I ride Herman onto the ferry to cross to the other side of the Rhine. The captain tells me that this is the first riding lawn mower he has ever transported in his long career as Rhine ferry commander, although, so he tells me, he has helped transport many other strange things, like an elephant and its circus. We philosophize for a while about what his ferry means for the trade of goods. The captain says it is in danger thanks to the Rhine bridge being planned by the local officials. That would be the end of the ferry—it would be a development that disfigures the landscape in exchange for quicker transport. "Not a very compelling trade-off," says the captain.

Herman and I continue on through the Franconian vineyards. It seems like the spring sun is illuminating the beauty of these romantic landscapes for the first time this year. I can't resist testing Herman's off-road capabilities and I'm surprised by how easily he handles the 30 percent incline in the muddy vineyards. I get into a conversation with a Mr. Lehmann, who owns a winery and would like to know why I'm making this racket on his estate. I jump at the opportunity to barter, but he seems to be too annoyed with Herman and me. At any rate, he declines to trade a barrel of wine for Herman, muttering that last year's harvest was poor, so the wine cellar is empty. I'm surprisingly relieved by his reaction; I've obviously become quite attached to Herman.

The next day I roll Herman out of the van in historic Rothenburg ob der Tauber. The prominent features of the town are its old city walls, high watch tower, and medieval houses. To the wonder of the tourists, Herman rattles by at nine in the morning, drives into the open door of a women's clothing store, and stops in front of a selection of skirts. It takes a little while for the visibly confused saleswoman to realize that it's not an accident or a rampage. I tell her about my dream to have a house in

Hawaii, and that she could support me in making my dream a reality with a generous clothing trade. Despite my pleading glance, she categorically rejects the offer on the grounds that she can't imagine a future for her and Herman. She requests that I engage the reverse gear immediately.

I begin to get the feeling that Herman is deciding our course. Shortly after, he drives over a bed of tulips in front of a used car dealership with his adjustable-height blades running. The sight of the mowed down tulips is heartbreaking. I'm stricken with grief as I explain to the owner that I don't approve of Herman's actions, either.

In the afternoon, Herman and I make a brief stop near Ravensburg when I notice a house where a psychic is plying her trade. I suddenly think it would be interesting to have psychic guidance on my upcoming visits through various bartering cultures. Maybe I'll get a few useful tips in the process.

Without telling her my plans, I ask the psychic what the future holds for me in a material sense. She sits in front of me, closes her eyes, and listens for the voices within her. A few moments later she suddenly and confidently says, "A large object!" I'm surprised that she mentions an object first, and I ask her if it could be a car. She closes her eyes and listens to her inner voice again. "The object is large and you can go inside it. Maybe a house!" she finally says as though it was the most normal thing in the world. Unbelievable! I had never before believed that psychics were real. In response to my question of how I can best acquire this house, she listens again and then advises me to follow my plans and strategies, but not to allow myself any long breaks. I'm impressed; I really hadn't expected that. The psychic strengthens my convictions. She thinks it's possible for me to achieve my goal—as long as I don't try to squeeze in a Caribbean vacation in the next 193 days.

In the evening, I reach the town of Wangen, where the local bartering ring is waiting for Herman and me in the community rec room. About thirty members sit behind tables covered in all sorts of objects for barter; mostly delicious treats, handmade items, and crafts.

Ms. Feustel, the leader of the group, explains that the unit of worth among the group is a "talent." The person offering an item places a numeric value on it based on the number of hours it took to produce it. An hour of work is worth ten talents. If someone would like to buy a homemade cake, they pay the forty talents that the cake costs or offers an item worth four hours of work in exchange.

Ms. Feustel tells me that this bartering ring has been around for over twenty years and that almost three hundred locals participate. I look around the room and see people of all ages, from children to old women. They all seem very happy that their way of bartering is getting the chance to be seen by all of Germany. Even if it all seems a little old fashioned, you can't overlook how excited everyone is to use their "talents" creatively. But I'm definitely surprised by how bureaucratic it all is. Before my visit, I had to fill out an official application for membership to get my own member number and pay my monthly dues of twelve Euros. Since something apparently went wrong with my money transfer, the woman at the cash box requests that I paid when I got there. Another woman holds some papers with barter numbers, talent account numbers, and other formulas under my nose. All this official paperwork for a one-time visit is a little bit much for me.

A short while later, Herman is the center of attention again. Ms. Feustel advertises his features through a microphone: five-gear speeds, reverse, adjustable height blades, maximum speed of five miles per hour. Reactions are tentative; they all probably have their own lawn-mowers at home. I have to keep my eyes on the prize, but I notice again how hard it is for me to part with Herman. I lean back and picture myself chugging along through the Swiss Alps with my friend, when suddenly someone raises their hand. It's the teacher at the local special needs school, as I later find out. He offers four hundred talents for Herman—forty hours of work for a lawn mower. From the reactions in the room, I can tell that that is a hell of a lot.

I gaze out at my travel companion parked in front of the building's glass storefront. He's waiting for me out there, and I'm in the midst of betraying our friendship. My heart almost breaks when I see tears rolling down Herman's right headlight, but it would be an unforgivable faux pas if I turned down such a high offer. Before I can even process what's happening, I see three schoolchildren jumping wildly around Herman, apparently looking for the gas pedal. It's done—I've traded him.

The next morning I transport him to the school, where the teacher offers me a donkey cart for the four hundred talents. The cart is clearly worth much more than Herman. I accept and set about hauling my new bartering item into the van with the students' help. No matter what we try, it doesn't fit—the massive hitch sticks far out of the open van. I won't be able to transport it like that. I suggest that we undo the whole exchange, but the children are already rattling around the lawn in front of the school. The teacher sees the tricky situation and calls the students over for a discussion. They decide that, instead, I can have the foosball table from the classroom and a small, blue plastic washing machine that is operated by turning a crank by hand. You could wash at most a pair of socks in it. I accept, relieved that I won't be crossing the Alps in a donkey cart. After everything is secured, I drive off, waving. Despite all the relief, the parting is sad. I have the feeling that Herman wants to say a clattering goodbye. I glance at his new home one last time in the rearview mirror and see how much fun the twelve-year-olds are having mowing the lawn in front of the school. And then I'm suddenly sure that this was the right trade.

2

MY FIRST NO

Austria

I drive over the border into Austria with the foosball table and the hand washing machine in my van. I stop in at another bartering ring in Vorarlberg, which Ms. Feustel had warmly recommended to me. I meet the leader, Mr. Müller, who proudly tells me that the principle of bartering is even more widespread here than with their friends in Wangen. According to Mr. Müller, a total of 150 shops and businesses in Vorarlberg are members of the bartering ring talent system, and accept both Euros and talents.

I decide to test it out right away. I head to a local bakery with my German bartering ring account, which still contains a few talents. I order breakfast and get a receipt with the price printed in Euros, and directly underneath it the price of 39.1 talents. I can choose how to pay. I'm shocked that this bartering idea is so accepted here. Next to me, a customer pays for her roll with her talent account. She explains that she uses this system to ensure the survival of local businesses, instead of shopping at large chains using Euros. She describes a closed bartering ring: a customer buys a piece of cake in a café and pays in talents. The baker then buys his flour from the flour producer, paying in talents, and also pays his employees in talents. The employees can then pay for cake in the café again.

I'm impressed; this real-life form of bartering makes sense. I know how important it is to support local business—I myself was born in a village of six hundred people in Sauerland, which still had its own baker, general store, and bank in the eighties. When I drive through the village today, I don't see a single shop. The residents have to drive over twelve miles to the next small town. There's simply no exchange of goods in the village anymore—the big chains in the neighboring town have made sure of that.

I would never have thought that a bartering ring thought up by the people could develop to this extent, but now that I know the advantages, I would take out all the annoying bureaucracy that comes along with it.

Eventually I meet ten interested people from the bartering ring in a parking lot in town. I show them the foosball table and the hand washing machine. In exchange, they offer me a portable pizza oven, folk music records, a talent coupon, and several local products.

Somehow none of the offered items really speak to me. I can't shake the feeling that a few well-meant local goods just won't get me closer to my goal. For the first time on this trip, I think about the way I've conducted trades so far. I've traded up in record time, achieving a considerable increase in worth—from a half-eaten apple to a foosball table, which must be three times that value. It's really just been a coincidence that the objects I received were worth more than my offering. I can't always assume that my counterpart will accept a trade for something that is worth less than his offer. It seems to have come to the point where I am the one who will receive less than I give. I will have to say no for the first time on my trip. I didn't make any plans in advance for dealing with this situation without offending anyone. The small crowd reacts in shocked silence when I explain that my goal is to continue to trade up so that I can achieve a dream I had thought was impossible. This sort of bartering does not seem to align with the group's beliefs. I try to lighten the mood by explaining and joking and finally shaking each member's hand apologetically, but I can't salvage this situation. I leave the parking lot and head toward Switzerland, feeling uneasy.

I spot a group of hikers as I drive over the top of a hill, and I get an idea. I pull the foosball table out of the van in the middle of a snowy field. Then I set myself up next to the table and shoot the hikers challenging glances. I draw a few humorous comments, but the majority of the group attempts to discreetly ignore the strange man playing a table game in the middle of nowhere. But then Dominik, my cameraman, decides to challenge me to a high altitude foosball duel. He destroys me mercilessly as we stand in the slippery snow. Despite my defeat, I'm glad to have the foosball table right now. I have to think of Hermann as I notice that it's so often the sentimental worth of a thing that makes it valuable, and how unimportant its material worth seems in these moments.

3

HELP, THE PLEIADIANS ARE COMING!

Switzerland

At the Swiss border, the customs officer nods his head toward my van, indicating that I should tell him what I'm transporting. I had plenty of time to prepare myself for this German-Swiss point of contact. I look him confidently in the eye and say what I think is the Swiss word for a foosball table. But apparently I should have studied my Swiss a little harder. The officer furrows his brow and makes the expression of a young man from a bad neighborhood in Berlin suggesting I hand over my wallet. My confidence melts away. After another meek attempt to repeat my vocabulary word, it seems that the German-Swiss exchange is over. He takes a look in the back of my van and tells his colleague that it's a foosball table worth no more than five hundred francs. He waves me through without making any further eye contact.

Once I arrive in Switzerland, I offer the table to passersby from inside my moving van (I've practiced my pronunciation), but I am met with little response. Finally, a woman directs me to the local inn, where the innkeeper is allegedly open to the idea of bartering. Unfortunately, I can't find the innkeeper, but I do notice that a row of pictures depicting UFOs is hanging on a wall. A neighbor answers my questions, explaining that the inn belongs to a group obsessed with UFO sightings, which sounds good to me; after all, I originally wanted to travel to the stars, not to Hawaii. Maybe this could be my chance to fulfill yet another dream.

I arrange a visit with the UFO group and convince the members to agree to an exchange of experiences. Before I know it, I'm standing in front of a picture of a UFO with Günter, Natan, Hans-Georg, and Patric. The members tell me that they are also in contact with the so-called Pleiadians, an anthropomorphic form of alien life that is millennia ahead of us in technological development. They inform me of an active trade between humans and Pleiadians, mostly in the form of advice from above, but they also trade very concrete things with the Pleiadians. So far this has gotten them an apple and a plum pit, the latter of which has grown into a stately tree in their garden. The men lead me to the courtyard, where a 24 x 16-inch stone provides an even more impressive example of intergalactic barter. According to Natan, this stone was hit with a laser beam by the Pleiadians from space. Nearby, a tree trunk is protected by Plexiglas—it has a very special meaning to the group, too. Natan explains that once, the group found a small hole in the tree trunk they think was shot with a laser gun.

Apparently, I look more skeptical than I realize, since Günter suddenly wants to make sure I know that the group doesn't have any sort of missionary goals, but rather that they have merely found a place here where they can share their beliefs.

Before our different positions on extraterrestrials can derail the conversation too much, I remember the reason for my visit and unload the foosball table. It's actually a relief that an object from this world unites us in our interests again and a spirited foosball game starts right away. After my offering has been thoroughly tested, I get down to business. I want to trade up again, yet at the same time the item has to be a more manageable size, so that it can fit on the plane to India next week. That's where I'll be visiting what is allegedly the oldest bartering market in the world.

The four men discuss what they can offer as a trade. I have the choice of a Swiss Army knife, an old wooden sled, and a coffee table book of UFO sightings—all appealing offers, but I suggest that they should throw in something very special. I express my interest in the stone that had allegedly been hit by an alien laser beam. The men wave it off: it's much too heavy, it won't inspire a cult in India, and above all, the stone belongs to them and it should stay that way. I'm not really surprised by their reticence, so I express interest in a smaller stone, about 4 by 2 inches in size, which is right next to its big brother and must have gotten a little bit of laser ricochet. The men discuss and debate back and forth until Hans-Georg gives the okay. I have to admit I'm the most excited about the little stone, even though it's already a good deal with all the other items.

With all my things packed up, I head out of Switzerland toward Frankfurt to get on my way to my second continent, where I plan to collect some more bartering knowledge. I think back on all the people and the crazy stories that I've experienced in the past two weeks—the tourist in Mainz who spontaneously traded for my bitten apple, and Serkan and David who were able to become such good friends in prison. I think of Hermann, who carried me so loyally and faithfully through the romantic German countryside (aside from mowing down a couple of tulips!). I think of the students and how excited they were to take Hermann for a ride around the schoolhouse, and of the quiet bartering ring in Vorarlberg and the men in the UFO group.

I reminisce in my hotel room: two weeks out of the two hundred planned days are gone and I've already bartered ten times. I got cigarettes for the apple, a book on Saarland for the cigarettes, a kitschy silver rabbit for that, then a first aid kit including scissors, a bottle of sherry in a lovingly crafted wooden box, fifty smoothies that constantly fell down, a waste barrel from an anti-nuclear power demonstration, then of course Hermann, who I traded for the foosball table and a blue hand washing machine, which finally got me a sled, a pocketknife, a coffee table book on UFOs, and the crowning item: the stone which had been shot by aliens. Ten trades in two weeks is pretty formidable, but it's still not a house in Hawaii.

Now, as I pause, I also notice how much the bartering has worn me out. I've been so infected by the bartering bug that I've hardly slept. If I want to make it through the next 187 days, I have to use my energy more efficiently. If I don't, I'll become a bartering burnout. I'll probably come up against entirely different challenges in India than I did in the German-speaking world. The donkey cart taught me that I also have to think about feasible transportation of my goods, especially in India, where I'll be traveling by train.

I also have to admit that despite my best intentions, the material worth of my items has decreased since Hermann. And what are Indians supposed to do with a book on UFOs, a wooden sled in the torrid heat, and a stone that other people think is proof of contact with extraterrestrials?

Despite all these thoughts, I'm still strangely excited to have gotten the stone. Maybe it's just the feeling that I've fulfilled a little bit of my childhood dreams of getting a little closer to the stars.

4

SLED MASALA

India

I find myself at the Frankfurt airport with my haul from ten days of bartering, ready to check in for my flight to southern India. The check-in lady at the desk attempts to remain serious as she places the sled on the conveyor belt. I notice how she keeps meeting her coworker's gaze and how she can hardly contain her laughter.

"I'm really looking forward to sledding in India!" I say casually. She grins at me and wishes me a fun trip.

Things are a bit more serious at the security checkpoint. The carry-on containing the hand washing machine is sent back and forth through the x-ray machine several times. I observe as several security guards attempt to interpret the bright colors on the screen. A short while later they escort me and the hand washing machine to a side room where a Frankfurt airport explosives expert goes over the appliance with a damp cloth attached to a plastic wand. I know the procedure from other flights. If the damp cloth changes color, I have myself a big problem. But of course that hasn't happened to me yet.

Unfortunately, the hand washing machine was manufactured in the sixties (you can tell from the black-and-white photograph of a beaming housewife with a tall hairstyle standing in front of a gray curtain in the instruction manual). So, obviously, the blue paint is also not the freshest; unfortunately, it turns the explosive detection cloth blue. There is now an astonished security officer standing in front of me, looking at the blue cloth. Clearly blue does not indicate explosives, and the officer seems to have never experienced the cloth turning unexpected colors. He quickly gets down to business:

"What is that?" the officer asks me, pointing stonily at the object in question.

"A hand washing machine . . . a blue one," I answer truthfully.

The security officer is silent for three seconds, and then looks at me: "Unusual, but not amusing. Have a good flight."

It quickly gets more amusing when I arrive in India. My first stop is Kochi, a metropolis in the southern Indian state of Kerala. The cab ride from the airport leaves no room for doubt that I have arrived in India. The driver careens through the narrow streets of the city, honking at anything that can move to the side. He pulls the steering wheel wildly from left to right, darting like a hunted fox not being chased by hunters. I sit in complete shock in the back seat and ask him to calm down. I still have a whole month to travel through India, so it really doesn't matter if I get to the hotel a minute earlier. The driver gives me a friendly grin and then turns on his flashers, too: *click click clickclickclick click.* He catches the morning pedestrians in his sight with the high beams and I see momentary overexposed images of people with wide open eyes and mouths, jumping out of the way of the turbo-taxi at the last second. It goes on like this: horn, lights, horn, horn, to the left side of the street, to the right side of the street, double horn, double lights along with double horn. When I climb out of the car in front of the hotel, I feel completely exhausted and terrified. What *was* that? A random occurrence, a drunken cab driver, or a completely normal bit of craziness in India?

I am staying for about a week in so-called Fort Kochi, the area of the city built by Portuguese colonists in 1503 and later expanded by the Dutch and English. The city on the little peninsula is bespeckled with Christian churches, sophisticated colonial buildings, and memorial sites for old conquerors like Vasco da Gama, but it is also surrounded by the wild, bustling Indian street life.

There are people on the street everywhere and at all times. Many are on bicycles or on tuk-tuks (motorized tricycles that are often used as taxis). There are busy-looking merchants and fishermen. I feel comfortable right away since the general atmosphere is laid back despite the great heat, even though I've heard many stories from my friends recalling pushy pedestrians driving everyone crazy with persistent service offerings. But aside from my cab driver, mutual respect and friendliness seem to be at the forefront here, even towards a European walking down the street with a sled and a hand washing machine.

But bartering doesn't seem to be working out so well. A fisherman and his colleague at the harbor are pulling in their big net, which is attached to a fifty-foot-tall wooden structure, and let out into the water on long poles. This is a very traditional way of catching fish that is still practiced here. I show the fisherman my objects for barter and he understands my intentions immediately, even though we don't speak the same language. I politely turn down the four-inch fish he offers me and continue on my way to find people with more to offer in trade: tuk-tuk drivers, fabric sellers, restaurant owners, and passersby. They all decline or can't offer me something of equivalent worth.

I advertise my goods artfully—I page through the UFO book with passersby and show them the photos of flying saucers over the Swiss mountains, hold the laser-struck stone up like a priceless holy object, and point toward the sky. Finally, I sit on the sled atop a steep sandy beach in Fort Kochi and slide down in front of many baffled Indians. The sled doesn't cut a bad figure as a surfboard in the wet sand. And the people watching my wondrous activities look silently, puzzled yet interested. They probably just think that a European must know what to do with a sled on the sand.

But what I also realize is that the Indians seem to be wise businesspeople. A carpet salesman explains bluntly that a sled is not going to be of much use when it's 95 degrees in the shade, he thinks the UFO book is fake, and the German rock is not rare, since the Europeans had already imported a huge amount of stones centuries ago to build their buildings. I hadn't expected this much practicality.

I still have one glimmer of hope: the hand washing machine. The carpet seller and many of the passersby enjoy the machine greatly. They want to understand exactly how it functions and they turn the crank with interest. I understand from my conversations that washing has an important cultural meaning in India. Even though some still wash in traditional ways by hand or in rivers, almost everyone on the street is wearing fresh clothing that smells wonderful. In this densely populated country with its 1.2 billion people (that's fifteen times the population of Germany), you can inconspicuously sniff the locals in the huge crowd, and they all smell lovely. I, on the other hand, feel a little grubbier. Most people have to shower or bathe every few hours in this heat. I only shower once a day and by the evening, I feel terribly uncomfortable. No later than three hours after I shower, I smell like sweat again and can start to see it on my clothing. Not the Indians: good smelling, clean clothes, and all in this heat and humidity. A hand washing machine must have some value.

As I somewhat elegantly ride the sled down a gravel pile among the bustle of Fort Kochi, I notice a wooden shed that reminds me of a kiosk. Big pieces of raw meat for sale hang from metal hooks in the beating sun. I offer the seller my items and ask if he will trade for the biggest piece of meat. (I admit that this decision could have been influenced by the unbelievable heat . . .) As we become more entangled in a communication jumble, fifteen to twenty Indian men have gathered around me, speaking frantically in languages I don't understand.

It then becomes clear that one of the men speaks English well—Amber, about forty years old and of course dressed in clean trousers and a blindingly white shirt (with no sweat stains). Understandably, he begins to interpret between me and the meat seller. He looks closely at the items I'm offering. The pocket knife gets his okay, he doesn't get the point of the UFO items, but as expected, the hand washing machine excites him. I squat in the middle of the enthusiastic group of men on the busy street, crank the washing machine, and indulge in grandiose explanations: "Look, this is so good, cleanest clothes possible, my friend. This is the best hand washing machine in Germany. You are always clean!"

I feel completely ridiculous, suddenly pitching washing machines in India while squatting on the ground between honking tuk-tuks and huge, raw chunks of meat. But the good feeling that breaks out among the men justifies my means. The men let themselves get carried away by my pitch. They all try the washing machine, laugh and talk. I think for a minute and then suggest five alternate uses for the hand washing machine:

Hand washing machine as plastic handbag—I hang the base of the machine over my arm and sashay past the men.

Hand washing machine as portable aquarium—I fill it with water and toss in a carrot to stand in for a goldfish. All the men stare at me uncomprehendingly.

Hand washing machine as lottery wheel—I throw a few newspaper clippings in the machine and then draw a winner.

Hand washing machine as soup pot—I fill it with water and spices and act out cooking without fire.

Hand washing machine as a message in a bottle—I toss the closed machine into the ocean in front of the men.

Before I even hear the splash, I know that I've gone too far. I've thrown my precious item into the ocean! The men around me become silent and look at me with concern. To save the situation, I grab the UFO book, sit on the floor among the standing men, and begin to read out loud in German:

"The first Pleiadians appear early in the morning with their spaceships over the snow-covered Swiss Alpine peaks. They are there again to prepare for another meeting. The Pleiadian ship lands slowly next to an apple tree."

Amber and the other men listen attentively even though they don't understand a word. They look at me with wide eyes as I read in an unknown language from a book full of photos of alleged flying saucers. It works. Amber steps forward and offers me a small piece of meat, about two pounds. I decline, since it is not equivalent to my items. Another half hour goes by on the street like that. I offer to wash Amber's clothing with the hand washing machine for the large piece of meat on the hook (six pounds), after retrieving the machine from the sea. It doesn't work. Only after Amber sees my distress at having wasted an hour and a half in the humid heat does he agree. He takes me over to the stand and tells the seller that he would like to buy the six-pound piece of meat for me. As soon as the big chunk of goat is packed in a plastic bag, he hands it over to me, beaming. I can hardly believe it! After working myself into a real bartering frenzy, the yes from Amber is totally unexpected.

I cheer and hug Amber over and over. What a crazy scene! The men standing around cheer with me, as though in addition to the current cricket world championship, India has also won the world cup and gold in all the Olympic sports. Everyone is euphoric. They page through the UFO book, one man turns the stone around and around in his hands, another tests the pocketknife out on the sled, and Amber turns around proudly with the hand washing machine. Totally exhausted, I sit down with my piece of raw meat in a drink shop and chug a liter of water. I take notice of how extremely tiring a bartering frenzy like that is. I look into my bag at the hunk of meat, which does not exactly appeal to me on a culinary level, and I see the flies that have landed on it in the midday heat. What have I done? The craziness of this trade hits me. If I don't want to be back at zero, I have to trade this piece of meat today. So I walk around and ask to trade with the cooks of the many open kitchens where food is being prepared in wok-like pans right at the dusty intersection. I don't have any success since none of the cooks speak English. Finally a tuk-tuk driver brings me to Burgar Street, where meat is always needed, as the name indicates. But all the restaurants discreetly decline the strange offer from the European. In an upscale tourist restaurant, the hostess escorts me, embarrassed but polite, discreetly to the door without introducing me to the cook.

Drained and exhausted, I meet a boy standing in front of a cooking school in the late afternoon. I tell him my story and he invites me to meet his aunt Maria who runs the school. I wait in a classy colonial building until a forty-year-old Indian woman appears, looking hesitant and skeptical. After a long explanation and carefully selected jokes to try to lighten the mood and inspire trust, she agrees to a trade, since she can use the meat for the cooking school. She offers me a plastic bowl in exchange. Images of Hermann, the foosball table, and the other items I've traded go through my head. I realize that I've gotten way off track since the bowl could be bought for fifty cents in the store next door. I carefully explain that my goal is to increase the value of my object. She seems to understand, so she adds in an electric juicer. After weighing the options for a long time, I decline with a heavy heart and leave the house.

I feel stressed. I'm at the bottom of the barter chain, so to speak. Why did I give up the foosball table? I wish I had driven to India through Turkey, Iran, and Afghanistan in a '68 hippie Volkswagen bus with the foosball table. Even though I know that idea is totally far-fetched, I'm so frustrated to be at the bottom after my start in India. I'm sitting here with a chunk of meat in front of a cooking school and watching flies land on it. I try to wave them away. They fly in a circle and calmly land on the meat again.

Suddenly, Maria's husband is standing in front of me. He leads me back into the school. Maria is in the kitchen and they are both looking happily at the kitchen table, where there is now a coffee maker next to the juicer. I'm moved by their excitement but most of all by the fact that they had thought about how to help me. Maria's husband tells me that it isn't easy to give up the juicer and the coffee maker, since many Indians can't afford such things. In fact, the coffee maker was imported from Canada. But, he explains, electricity in the state of Kerala is excessively expensive, so they can never use these appliances, and that's why they decided to make the generous offer. I'm so thankful to have met these nice people. I make the deal and shake both of their hands.

The next day, I visit them again to see the meat become a good smelling meal being served to two Japanese tourists.

In the Valley of Trading Tears

I'm accompanied by the coffee machine and the electric juicer as I drive to the tea hills of Munnar with Saneer, a twenty-four-year-old Indian taxi driver. Munnar is a region at an altitude of 3,300 feet, consisting of green hills completely covered in tea plants. These hills, which shine in green all the way to the horizon, are an unbelievable sight. They look as if they are covered in moss.

But before I see this beautiful landscape, I have to endure Indian Street Traffic School, part two. Saneer seems to have decided to make the five-hour drive over a heavily traveled route in half an hour. Like the airport cab driver before him, he races like a crazy person through the traffic, quickly passing everything that his car is capable of passing. The occupant of the next lane is also completely unimportant to him, whether it's another car, a semi-truck, or a car with a motorcycle trying to squeeze by next to it. I still don't know how Saneer managed to make it through the cars; I only know that he put the pedal to the metal.

I'm getting scared, so I ask him to drive more carefully. He laughs and says only, "European people, always afraid!" Okay, I get it. I've been labeled a European sissy simply because I don't believe in reincarnation and would rather not end my life today. Saneer continues driving cheerfully. Left, right, down the middle, honk, intersect two cars, stop short, tailgate. After half an hour, I still don't understand the system behind it all, but I gradually realize that the insanity always seems to work out okay. While executing a passing maneuver between a tuk-tuk and a truck, Saneer explains that he did hit a (sacred) cow once, but otherwise he's never had any trouble. Somehow my fear dissipates, probably because my body can't produce any more adrenaline, and I relax and accept the high-speed zigzagging. After a while, I start to get brave. I ask Saneer if he can take his hands off the wheel for three seconds. He does it and laughs. I up the ante: "Five seconds!" Saneer really does it. After the five seconds, I ask him to end his attempt. He probably would have played "hands-free drive up the switchbacks to Munnar" with me. I didn't try it.

The chances of dying from this style of driving are actually not very low. India holds the sad world record for accidents: an unbelievable one hundred thousand people die on the roads every year and an additional two million are badly injured each year, so some approximation of European driving habits could be beneficial.

The moss-like tea hills and the fresh mountain air in Munnar relax me. I walk through the hills with my coffee maker and juicer looking for bartering partners working on the plantations carrying big sacks of tea on their backs, like I've seen in photos. But unfortunately, there is no one walking around here. Saneer tells me that it isn't possible to visit tea factories, since the tea companies don't let anyone into their production facilities. We go to the city's tea museum to look for a deal. The guard asks us to go to the regional government office of the city to get official authorization—this isn't much of a surprise in ultra-bureaucratic India.

And so, we sit in the regional office in front of an Indian official who is stamping papers under a fan and in front of a computer from the early nineties. I explain my bartering project and he sends us back to the museum. Back at the museum, another man tells us that the local office, not the regional office, is responsible for the authorization.

And so an hour I sit, annoyed, in a huge room at the local office. This one also has many officials, fans, and computers from the early nineties, but this time, the officials are drinking tea and not stamping anything. I'm called into an office where the boss is waiting for me. While I explain my bartering project and my dream house in Hawaii, he is kneeling next to his desk in front of his printer, which is indiscriminately swallowing and tearing papers. While he fights with the machine, the head of the office repeats, "Hm, hm. Yes, yes," but doesn't seem to absorb anything I tell him. He only has eyes for the printer.

After I finish my explanations, he stands up, shakes my hand, and directs me to the regional office. I want to explain that I've already been there, but the door is already closed, and the official is on the other side of it.

So we go back to the regional office. The same official that we met several hours ago now says that he is responsible for the authorization, but does not want to issue it to me. I pull myself together even though I feel angry enough to burst. I exit wordlessly.

Outside, I wait for Saneer to get the car. As I sit there with my elbows on the juicer and coffee maker, a tuk-tuk driver comes by and shows some interest in the items. His name is Justin, seems jolly, and starts talking business. He asks how much tea I want for the appliances. I say twenty pounds, he says ten, I say eighteen, he says ten, I say sixteen, he says ten, I say fourteen, he says ten, I say twelve, he says ten and sticks out his hand for me to shake. As I hesitate, he grabs my hand. The deal is done. I'm extremely annoyed that I let him pull a fast one on me. But a deal's a deal. Justin buys the ten pounds of tea for me in the store next door, enough for a thousand cups of tea. I'm not really happy with this development, since ten pounds of tea doesn't have much worth in Munnar. At the very least, I would like to know what was to become of the objects I just gave up.

So I ride with Saneer and Justin on his tuk-tuk through the endless tea hills. Since I made such a bad trade, I am allowed to drive the tuk-tuk as consolation. At first the motorized tricycle stalls, but then I get a feeling for the clutch and I enjoy the pretty drive through the hills. During a pit stop, Justin tells me that the tea hills were laid out centuries before by English colonists. He says that his ancestors traded the tea to the English and often got only rice and water for an entire harvest, which they hardly managed to live on. Today the tea hills belong mostly to the Indian conglomerate TATA, which seems to own half of India between its various branches. Since Justin's wife works for the company, they get a little house, health insurance, and thirty euros a week, which he is very satisfied with.

A short time later, we reach Justin's village in the tea hills. There doesn't seem to be any other European visitors. The village children jump on me excitedly and wonder about my appearance and height. The aforementioned house appears to be a two-room cottage, six feet tall, with two beds for four people in one of the small rooms. We stand in front of the coffee maker and juicer with the village children in the bedroom/dining room. Justin grins widely. He can't hide his pride at having made such a good exchange with a European. Many curious faces look through the door into the room. It's very disappointing to discover that the coffee machine has a US plug that doesn't fit in the electrical socket. Saneer jumps in right away and fashions a makeshift converter from two wires, so that we can see the water run through a filter made of newspaper into the coffee pot. The amazed faces of the children tell me that there isn't much coffee here in the middle of the tea plantations.

At the end of the afternoon, I ask Justin if he is happy with his simple life. He answers that he can't imagine anything better. I'm struck by how little happiness has to do with wealth.

A few days later, I finally arrive by tuk-tuk at supposedly the biggest bartering market in the world, which is supposed to be two hundred years old: Matta Chanda, my real destination here in India.

After a bumpy ride, the "only, first, world's biggest and most grandiose bartering market in the world" is there before me in the midday heat: a few shabby carnival stands in rows, selling inflatable neon dolphins, streamers, and firecrackers. That's all? And the price tags on the goods shine at me in all the neon colors of the world. I'm completely disappointed. I would like to throw my ten pounds of tea down in the middle of the carnival market and shout, "Barterman is here, let's barter! Strange, world's greatest bartering market, come out now!" But the presence of Krishna, the friendly organizer, leaves me no room for an emotional outburst. He tells me that he has never heard of the market being big, great, unique, and bartering-friendly, as the Internet says. I tell him that I traveled specifically to India because of the reports about bartering here. Krishna can hardly refrain from grinning at my naive Internet research. He explains to me that there hasn't been bartering at this market for one thousand years, because India is a modern country and people prefer to use money. He calmly explains that bartering is the inferior system and that you always have to carry the exact product that another person happens to need. Oh, no, I think, but I don't say anything. Krishna finally wishes me well on my bartering journey, and I leave the market with an inflatable neon dolphin I bought for ten rupees.

A few days later, I'm lying on the bunk in an Indian train heading toward Goa, the erstwhile hippie enclave of the late sixties and seventies. I've moved past the disappointment over the famous Matta Chanda market. I look at the framed picture of Hawaii that I brought with me from Germany while I lie on the five-and-a-half foot bunk in the third level of the open compartment, under loud fans and in front of windows consisting only of bars. In the midst of the huge amount of noise created by my fellow passengers, I wonder earnestly if my plan for a house in Hawaii is actually realistic. Ten pounds of tea lie under my scrunched legs. The tea has begun to annoy me. How am I going to get a dream house from tea? It seems impossible.

The next morning, I go through the train and speak to Indian families, showing them the tea and the Hawaii hula-hula picture with its flower frame. The reactions are very guarded; a polite smile is a signal for me to move on. Only two backpackers in the thirty-car train understand my story and find it funny, but they can't offer me any more than a two euro-dollar coin.

Tuk-tuk Mania

After a thirty-two-hour ride, I exhaustedly step off the train in Magao in the state of Goa. I'm greeted by a horde of tuk-tuk drivers who want to show off their vehicles. I let myself get drawn in to their over-the-top pleas. Naturally, each person's tuk-tuk is the best. The drivers tell me that each tuk-tuk has a name, like "Linda" or "Krishna" or "Mahandra." I can't help but think of Hermann, how I too gave my lawn mower a name, and how much fun I had had with the newly christened Hermann.

And suddenly I know just what I want. I want to own a tuk-tuk! It will be a great help if I have a concrete goal on my path toward my house in Hawaii. I won't just aimlessly trade this or that; I will trade this sack of tea for a tuk-tuk. I will just politely decline any other offers.

Yeah, I won't accept anything less than a tuk-tuk! With this goal in mind I stay for a week in Anjuna, *the* hippie enclave in Goa. Apparently, many expats still live here. If you Google "Anjuna," you'll find tons of pictures of groups of naked hippies mugging for the camera. I've also figured out what to do after I get my tuk-tuk—I'll style it into a hippie mobile and offer it to one of these expats for something more valuable.

I first meet Mark, an Indian journalist in his fifties who lives in a red house next to my hotel. The salesgirl in the corner shop had pointed to that house when I asked her who owned the old tuk-tuk on the corner. Now I am standing before Mark's door. I hear Pink Floyd blaring through the door. *Excellent*, I think. *A guy like this will definitely be into bartering.* Inside, Mark—who speaks perfect English and wears a beach hat and his shirt untucked—tells me that he is only renting it. The owner of the house and the tuk-tuk is Dirk, a German expat who had to travel to Bangkok because of problems with his visa.

As we talk, Mark opens two beers to accelerate the getting-to-know-you process. In the midday heat, the alcohol goes right to my head and I have some trouble following his long stories and processing all the information. Mark tells me how he used to live in Bali but had to leave because he had said something politically incorrect about certain residents of the island in a documentary. He tells me lots of stories about women, about long evenings with Dirk, about Dirk's wild lifestyle, and that he could certainly arrange the tuk-tuk deal. I'm relieved and euphoric, even though Mark talks faster and faster until I can't keep up anymore.

Later, Mark writes Dirk an email clarifying my trade offer, and explains to me that I'd have to offer a few services to Dirk along with the tea, such as sweeping the house. After a few more beers, Mark offers to make the tuk-tuk deal himself if Dirk doesn't get back to him. But anyway, he's sure that Dirk won't have any problems with the idea.

Two more days go by. I feel like I've checked my email four hundred times—refresh, refresh—but I only get emails from Perry, Cherry, or Merry who want to sell me Viagra, and not from Dirk. He remains silent.

I begin to fear that Mark has promised too much. I visit him again and once more the beer flows in the midday heat. Mark assuages my fears: Dirk will definitely reply. He starts to talk again about women, his work as a journalist, and beer. No concept of the idea that I might want to say something; the man is completely in monologue-mode. It's really all too much for me, but I stay because he said he would trade me the tuk-tuk himself if it came down to it. An evening at a beach bar follows, and then another at a night market. The monologues annoy me more and more. Whenever I buy a soda, he comments, "Oh, Michael's getting a soda!" and when I eat a bag of chips, he says, "Oh, chips are good!"

Mark is educated and very nice, but the one-sidedness of the conversation makes the relationship unbearable. It's been thirty hours since the email to Dirk went out, and despite Mark's reassurances, I no longer believe that he is going to respond. I ask Mark if he is still willing to trade the tuk-tuk himself; I offer him endless services in exchange. Mark reacts with perturbation and annoyance. He doesn't remember any of that and he looks mad. Apparently he only made that offer while drunk—I shouldn't have taken it seriously. I'm completely stressed out. For two days I let myself be bombarded by his monologues and now I have nothing to show for it. I leave Mark behind, a knot of frustration in my stomach. The first thing I need is a good night's sleep before I can stomach more of the eternal rambling.

The next day, I decide to talk a walk along a bit of the dreamy Ajuna Beach, trying my luck in the many beach bars. Of course, the first person I meet on the beach is Mark, who immediately starts back at the beginning, assuring me that Dirk will get in touch soon and that I really didn't need to look for another tuk-tuk. His rambling is making my blood boil so I decline another invitation for a midday beer. He doesn't care at all about the matter at hand; he's just looking for a victim to submit to his endless flow of words. I move on and I don't see him again.

In a beach bar not three hundred feet further, I meet Michel, an old German hippie who came here in the seventies and stuck around. He wears striking red glasses, has short blond hair, and looks fit despite his heavy consumption of cigarettes. "An hour of swimming every morning!" he replies to my unasked question.

Then he talks about free love and that no one belongs to anyone else here. He also tells me that hippies used to barter regularly and money didn't play a big role. He emphasizes that bartering was never seen as something special; it was completely normal. No one would have thought of bartering as something unique to hippie culture.

Then Michel tells me about the communication gap between him and his son, who is thirty-four like me, and lives a middle-class life in Germany working in the IT field. He tells me that it is often uncomfortable for his son that his father lives as an old hippie in Goa, even though he hasn't had just hippie friends for a while. He is actually invited to a friend's party that's coming up, and the friend is a millionaire. But as usual, Michel's son would rather avoid contact with his father.

Michel takes a deep drag of his Indian cigarette, which he relights repeatedly with an oversized lighter. He looks out at the ocean quietly and contemplatively. I get the feeling that a fascinating person is sitting next to me, who thirty years ago had the courage to travel far from home to try a completely new way of living. But he certainly had not foreseen the consequences of his departure.

I continue on my way under the midday sun with my sack of tea on my shoulders, since Michel has no tuk-tuk that he can trade. I stop in front of a group of beach huts that tower over the beach on high bamboo poles. I climb up one of the ladders. In one of the huts, I meet Toas, a fashion designer from Berlin who is a few years younger than me. With his short hair and dressed only in an orange tulle scarf, Toas makes me think of an Asian monk. He doesn't have a tuk-tuk to offer, but he trades me two pounds of tea for a portable speaker.

I continue to the next beach bar with my tea and speaker. The now eight pounds of tea and the speaker get heavier and heavier in the heat.

I would love to throw the whole collection into the ocean. Despite the fascinating people I meet on the beach, the excitement of bartering is not much fun anymore. How am I going to get out of the Valley of Tears this time?

At the next beach bar I talk to Christopher, a French expat. You can see his wild life on him. He is maybe forty, but his skin looks lived-in, and he's missing a few teeth. He works here doing tandem paragliding for tourists. Before I know what's happening, we are tandem paragliding high in the air over Anjuna Beach. It's a once in a lifetime view: long sandy beaches, palm forests, and the wide open ocean with the sun glinting off it. Up in the air, Christopher tells me that he worked as an engineer in his country's nuclear program, and so in a sense he contributed to the creation of weapons. He tells me how he made a lot of money, but happily traded wealth for freedom on this hippie beach. As we glide in a zigzag over the beach, he explains that he has just a few rupees in his wallet, but he's high up in the air every day and much happier than before. He laughs when I ask if a little bit of money wouldn't increase his happiness just a bit, and he says that his Iranian girlfriend is rich enough.

Since Christopher also doesn't know where I could get a tuk-tuk, I begin to call around, making contact with people for whom it wouldn't be a big financial burden to trade a tuk-tuk. I call Sabine, a friend from Cologne, who gives me the number for Wiebke, who is biking through India. Wiebke gives me the number of Tamara, who lives in Goa, and Uti, who apparently came here from Germany decades ago.

The many telephone conversations and their never-ending questions about my bartering plan are tiring, but I finally receive an invitation to visit Uti. Mark, the journalist in the red house, had also mentioned Uti to me in one of his soliloquies. Apparently, he had rented from her until there was some sort of scandal. From Mark and Wiebke I also know that Uti is rich. So I head out to meet her with high hopes.

I sit on the terrace of an extravagant colonial house and tell Uti my plan. At the end I pose the question: Does she know anyone who would trade a tuk-tuk for eight pounds of tea and a speaker if I threw in some sort of service, too, like butler duties?

Unfortunately, Uti doesn't seem interested in my idea at all. Instead, she tells me about when she came to Goa twenty-five years ago as a young woman and ended up at an LSD party. Because of her gold dress, everyone at the party thought she was a "Golden Girl," and in their intoxicated states, they actually prayed to her. Years later, hippies in the streets of Goa still reverently address her as "Golden Girl," even though she long since left the hippies for the upper class.

Even though I find Uti's story entertaining, I notice that my thoughts are stuck on tuk-tuks. The only thing going through my head is who I can contact to achieve my goal. I catch myself smiling and nodding even though I am only absorbing snippets of her words. As Uti continues talking, I suddenly remember that Michel, the old German hippie, had mentioned a party with his German friend and millionaire. Once I'm out of Uti's house, I call Michel right away. "Sure, come along. Armin has a company in southern India and he's always up for crazy ideas!" Michel says, and a huge weight lifts from my shoulders.

Upon my arrival at the three-story estate with its expensive furnishings, I am politely greeted by several Indian maids. A German in his mid-forties suddenly shouts over the balcony:

"Hey, the Bartering King is here, and early. I should tell you that Armin doesn't like that!"

I climb the stairs to the party and am snubbed again when I try to shake the man's hand.

"Oh, the Bartering King doesn't think it's important to take his shoes off on the expensive floors!"

I feel pretty alienated. Armin of course accompanies it all with too-loud laughter, but even if it is meant as a joke, I can't laugh about it.

About ten more guests arrive, all Germans. A conglomeration of people enters: German hippies like Michel, short-term expats like the bodybuilder Uwe, and his rugby mate Roger, and German emigrants to India like Christine, who has been organizing social aid projects for twenty years. She tells me about her youth in Germany, which was partly spent on the streets. Armin takes each guest through his lavish house filled with worldly furniture and tells us what was newly acquired. To top it all off, he gets a particularly old wine from the cabinet and presents it to the guests so sensationally that everyone raises their glass to him.

I sit next to Armin to give our trade a chance despite the less than promising start. Before I can finish a sentence, he starts talking over me, leaning toward me from an ornately carved mahogany armchair. Loudly, so that all the guests can hear, he asks:

"Hey, are you on Facebook?"

"Yeah, of course. Why?"

"Because everyone on Facebook is completely crazy."

"Why?"

"They make themselves into slaves for Facebook, and all their info is everywhere."

"I know it's not a problem, since Facebook . . ."

"Quit bull****ing. You're completely crazy!"

After this conversation, it is clear that no tuk-tuks will be traded this evening, but unfortunately, Armin has not reached the zenith of his contemptuousness. A while later I am sitting next to Christine, who is telling me about her life as an expat in India, when Armin commands me to stand up so he can talk with her.

"Give the boss his chair!"

I stand up so that I don't get thrown out. The absurd scene here is too interesting. I tell myself silently not to take anything personally, that the bartering plan is just a game and these people aren't my friends. I make it through the evening with the proper emotional distance, observing how German expats should definitely not behave.

Again, Armin shows his three Indian maids and the majority of his guests who has the money and who calls the shots. He even loudly cautions his buddy Achim in front of everyone.

"You're always too nice to people, so don't come back!"

Achim responds with an intimidated grin, but tries to give as good as he gets.

"Yeah, don't forget that only one person is allowed to talk in Armin's house."

I listen to the slurred conversation of an old hippie couple, about sixty years old and from Munich.

"Badass party yesterday. Man, we were high."

"Yeah, it was totally cool!"

I know this conversation all too well from my friends and myself, when we were in our early twenties. To hear that out of the mouths of potential grandparents makes me thinks that a certain maturity is missing here.

A mother sits next to me with her two pubescent children. At some point she rolls a joint and brings the kids out to Armin's new balcony to smoke. A short while later the daughter is making out with her boyfriend on the bed in the next room. Michel gets up in arms, telling Armin that he won't accept this orgy happening in the next room. Armin laughs loudly.

"Let them have fun. We all want to have fun. Not to mention, swingers clubs are still the best place to make a good trade!"

He looks at me as he laughs cynically at his play on my talk of barter and exchange. I counter by telling him that he clearly has no idea what a real exchange is. But he talks right over me. I do it too. "Let me talk!"

Before I finish the sentence, he is talking over me again. I retort immediately.

"Let me talk if you want to have a discussion!"

Armin mumbles something indiscernible to himself while grinning doubtfully.

I leave the house a little later without saying goodbye. I look around and see Armin up on the roof lighting ostentatious fireworks and laughing loudly as the guests applaud.

Back at the hotel I no longer have the energy to think about tuk-tuks. How did I get roped into this when I just wanted to barter for something? I had imagined Goa as a loving place with old-school hippies who lived with humanity and mutual trade. But apparently I only meet people who use this place as a platform to boost their image.

After I have digested the experience somewhat, I decide to contact Tamara, who is riding her bike through India. And Tamara even has a potential trade partner to introduce me to. So I head off toward Palolem Beach in southern Goa. I'm relieved to have my back toward Anjuna and leave behind this depressing leg of my bartering blitz.

I meet Tamara in a beach bar where she introduces me to Panta, a fifty-three-year-old Indian man who reminds me of a guru. He seems very relaxed, speaks rather quietly and carefully, and has this constant contented smile on his face.

We get right to the point. Panta asks me what's up for trade. I tell him about my desire to trade for a tuk-tuk and show him the eight pounds of tea and speaker. As he watches me with an amused grin, I notice Tamara next to him. She seems to be judging my request rather critically. She interjects that it doesn't necessarily have to be a tuk-tuk, and it would be okay for Panta to decide himself what he would like to trade. I deny that immediately. I don't want to make Panta uncertain after he was so receptive to my offer. I wish Tamara wasn't so critical, even though I am of course thankful that she introduced me to him. So I reply that it is very important to me that the next item I receive is a tuk-tuk, or else I would never climb out of this rut.

"Yes, I can understand that!" says Panta, nodding.

Tamara holds her stance that it doesn't necessarily have to be a tuk-tuk in exchange for some tea. Maybe Panta could trade something else first, something smaller. I give her a friendly nod, but on the inside I'm almost ready to burst. How can this woman, who introduced me to the first person in Goa earnestly interested in trading, tell him not to trade a tuk-tuk? I take the risk of appearing rude to her, since I will never get this chance again. I explain to Panta that I can throw some services in with the tea and speaker; for example, I can appear in his yoga center for two days as a clown. Panta smiles serenely. He seems to appreciate my dedication and nods.

"Yes, why not a tuk-tuk? I like your ideas. But I certainly do not need a clown in the yoga center!"

I'm so relieved by this quick agreement that I immediately throw in more. I offer to produce a promotional video for his yoga center. He nods, I reach out my hand, we shake, and even Tamara nods in surprised approval.

I've done it! After nine miserable days of searching for a tuk-tuk trade, the object of my desires is almost close enough for me to touch—at least I think so.

I agree to present Panta with a detailed script the next day so that he can get an idea of how I envision the promotional video to look. For the rest of the day I sit at my computer, giving my all to think of a structure for the video. The next morning, I proudly lay almost four pages of ideas on the table in front of him.

Panta looks through them calmly, then grins in his serene, guru-like manner and says, "That is not what I am looking for."

He explains that he would like a video about his vision as a spiritual leader and not about his yoga center. I'm frustrated but I don't let on. Instead, I promise to have a new script ready by the next day.

The next day at eleven, Panta goes through my new script, which I compiled based on the informational material about his goals, mindset, values, and visions, gives me his guru grin, and says that it's what he was looking for. I'm unbelievably relieved and suggest shooting right away. He shakes his head and tells me that he will need three days in peace to prepare himself to film. I explain that three days out of two hundred is a bitter loss when in the midst of a bartering blitz, and I ask him to move up the shooting. Panta reacts with irritation. He waves me off and disappears into his home without mincing words.

You can imagine the next three days as me pacing aimlessly around my hostel room. Sure, in front of the hostel there is a gorgeous beach with palm trees and bars, but I just can't relax. I can't help thinking about how fast the days are going by and how quickly my time for this bartering blitz is running out. And if I don't accomplish my mission, I'll have to return to Berlin empty handed, chalking up this project as "at least I tried."

Of course the daily life that awaits me in Berlin is much more structured than the one I have now. But imagining moving into a house in Hawaii at the end of this adventure is obviously enticing. I would love to enjoy the warmth in Hawaii during the winter months instead of slipping on an icy street in five-degree weather. I have to do it. I'm hugely determined, so this waiting period is torture. Time is running through my fingers.

When the three days are finally over, I feel drained and stressed; Panta is relaxed and cheerful with his white turban on his head. He starts the day with a few jokes while flirting with some female visitors at his yoga center.

We finally film the video, edit it, and the next day it is approved. Panta likes the result. He takes the tea and the speaker and leads me to the entrance of the yoga center.

Tuk-tuk Trauma

The sight that greets me makes me first think that someone has abandoned their broken-down tuk-tuk in front of the door. Before I can complain to Panta about the bad habit of Indians just tossing all their garbage and rubbish in the street, he points to the tuk-tuk and hands me a key. Oops, so that's our deal, I think. I try to seem excited about this tuk-tuk even though it has seen better days. It is black with a lot of rust on the back and the canvas roof is torn, but Panta assures me that it drives really well. What can I do but believe him?

I sit down in it to try it out right away. The vehicle is started by some sort of iron rod on the left that you have to jerk upwards. I try it. Nothing happens. I try about twenty times, and then my arm hurts too much.

Two young yoga center visitors who are excitedly chatting with Panta look over at me in irritation. The noise from the broken tuk-tuk is disturbing their conversation with the guru. I try to lighten the mood with a silly grimace, but the two women's expressions do not change. A guy with a loud, smelly tuk-tuk right in front of the entrance to the yoga center does not fit their idea of a wellness retreat in India. They turn away from me. Panta, on the other hand, seems to feel for me. He grins and indicates that I should keep trying, but he does keep his distance along with the women (Perhaps a good idea, in case the tuk-tuk explodes.)

After another five minutes, the thing finally springs to life, clattering loudly. The two girls ignore this surprising turn of events. They are very busy writing down their addresses in Europe for Panta. I step on the gas, but the tuk-tuk only goes backwards! I pull the clutch with all my strength, but I can't manage to change the direction. I stop and start backwards slowly until I'm right in the middle of the entrance to the yoga center. Panta gives a friendly wave and discreetly disappears into the building with the two students. I don't know how, but I eventually find the forward gear and sputter slowly toward the hostel. As expected, the drive is difficult. I'm bowled over by honking Indian drivers, the tuk-tuk continuously stalls, I'm not used to driving on the left, and I can hardly manage the balance between gas and clutch. What have I done to myself? I desired a tuk-tuk so much and for so long. And now I'm sitting in an rusty pile of junk that I can hardly drive. My initial euphoria at achieving this stopover goal suddenly becomes panic. I'm overcome with fear that I'll never reach my goal.

The next day I decide to look toward the future again. I buy spray paint in gold, silver, white, and black and orange PVC film. It's time to pep up the tuk-tuk a bit, at least visually, if I want to be able to trade it. After just a few hours, it looks eye-catching and eccentric. All the rust and dirt is gone. I replaced the broken, black roof with the bright orange PVC. The paint job—gold, silver, white, and black stripes—has turned it into a real space-looking tuk-tuk. Even during the styling, Indians continually gather around me and the tuk-tuk to watch in amazement. They tell me that they have never seen anything like it among the countless black and yellow tuk-tuk taxis. I'm relieved. I have something that's one of a kind!

A bit later I drive my space tuk-tuk through Palolem Beach and get a lot of attention and approval from both locals and vacationers. Waving and laughing passersby greet me with a thumbs-up as the space tuk-tuk passes by on its maiden voyage. Thanks to my driving practice, I can now keep it chugging along for more than five minutes at a time.

On my way from Palolem Beach to the neighboring town, my tuk-tuk gives up again among the fields and palm trees. I pull the starter rod on the left with all my strength ten times, twenty times, thirty times. But it doesn't help. No more noise comes from the tuk-tuk. A little later, a few motorcyclists help me push-start the tuk-tuk in the midday heat, but that doesn't help either. The space tuk-tuk falls silent and still. We try three more times, until I sit down on the country road in the 95-degree heat, sweating and panting and damning the tuk-tuk. My fresh shirt, which I put on especially for the official maiden voyage, is soaked through. I'm frustrated and devastated to realize that this tuk-tuk won't bring me any good. One of the men who helped me push takes pity and calls a mechanic for the frustrated European on the side of the road. The mechanic hauls the tuk-tuk away a little later and repairs it.

It's become more than clear that this tuk-tuk will not win any prizes in a bartering competition. As fun as it looks, it's actually old and in need of repairs. Who would want to trade for it? Every Indian taxi driver knows these motorized tricycles well and would know that it wasn't good for much and was visually no longer the norm for a taxi, either.

I start to curse myself out of frustration. What was I thinking with this paint job?

I decide to lean on my contacts again, and go through the list of people who can help me in this situation: Wiebke, Sabine, Tamara, Uti, Mark, Michel, etc. In my panic I call without discretion and ask everyone who I already asked about getting me a tuk-tuk if they would like to make another trade. Everyone enjoys the phone calls—except me.

Wiebke is the one who is finally able to help. She'll talk to her colleague Kalian, who is from the southern Indian metropolis of Bangalore and has a hot connection to a silk manufacturer. He calls me up a short time later and tells me that he finds my bartering blitz exciting, and that he would like to trade some silk for the tuk-tuk. I'm relieved and elated. I didn't think I'd find a trade so quickly, and especially not over the phone. After all, the silk manufacturer hasn't even seen the space tuk-tuk yet. But unfortunately, there is always some bureaucratic hurdle or another in India that can quickly eliminate options. I already experienced that in the tea hills of Munnar.

It's the Indian bureaucracy that stands between the space tuk-tuk and the silk manufacturer 370 miles away in Bangalore. As a potential helper, I contact Raj, the head of a travel agency and cargo transporter. He tells me that tuk-tuks may not be transported across state lines. A tuk-tuk from Goa can only be driven in Goa and a tuk-tuk from Kerala can only be driven in Kerala. No ifs, ands, or buts. Cross the border once and the fun is over, no exceptions—especially if the owner is not a resident of India and the tuk-tuk was bartered instead of purchased. It's obvious that I have no chance of getting this tuk-tuk to the silk manufacturer. It's hard enough to put my bartering ideas into practice due to the unexpected difficulties between different cultures. My project seems like a huge wall that I am looking up at in doubt, which gets higher when I manage to climb up a little.

I lament my problems to Raj again and he actually understands my troubles with Indian customs, since he has had a lot of contact with Europeans and understands their point of view. He has sympathy for me. After a long discussion about the dead end I'm in, he actually offers to take the tuk-tuk himself to sell later. Then he calls the silk manufacturer in Bangalore and orders me as much silk as he can get for the estimated worth of the tuk-tuk, to be paid with his own money. I should now be able to travel to Bangalore to pick up the silk. I remain reserved and cautious. How do I know that all the parties involved will remember this conversation in two days? How do I know that the silk manufacturer fully understood Raj's request? And how do I know that unforeseen circumstances won't change the situation completely?

In the Heart of India: Silk, Poverty, and Six Years of Drought

In spite of my doubts, I board the night bus toward Bangalore and sleep out my exhaustion from the last few days on a bunk without a pillow or blanket. After a long drive through the night, I make a late morning pit stop in Hampi. In an area of over ten square miles, there is an incalculable number of temples, which all beg to be visited. Between the 14th and 16th centuries, Hampi was the capitol city of the important Hindu kingdom of Vijayanagar and had almost half a million residents in its golden age. Today, only about two thousand people live in the city, and they have some strange and unpleasant cohabitants. On every temple, there are hordes of monkeys overrunning the place.

When I retrieve my Hawaii picture with the house, hula-hula girl, and flower frame from my backpack to compare the state to Hampi, a monkey immediately swipes the photo from my hand. An intense tug of war begins between us over the Hawaii dream house. What does this monkey want with it? Doesn't he have a home already? The interesting part for him actually seems to be the plastic flowers that decorate the frame. The tug of war ends when he realizes that the flowers taste pretty bad and the picture isn't so sexy with bite marks on it. I'm pretty annoyed by this monkey. That picture was supposed to accompany me as motivation toward my end goal—every time I looked at it, all of my difficulties paled in comparison to what awaited me. Now the flowers look more like dried-up weeds from a grave that haven't been watered in a week. Too bad.

That's how the first day of my bartering trip dedicated solely to sightseeing comes to an end. Even if the picture is destroyed, I enjoyed the day. For the first time in weeks I treated myself to a little vacation and actually relaxed.

But then it's time for me to jump on the next bus, and I arrive in the southern Indian metropolis of Bangalore twenty hours later. I take a taxi to the silk factory. During the drive, my driver tells me about the living conditions in the region. He tells me that it hasn't rained here in six years and that this is one of the poorest areas in India. Just a glance out the window is the proof of his statements: parched landscapes and poverty everywhere. The gutters look like garbage dumps and sewers. Instead of the many cars that populate Goa, here I almost only see people riding bicycles. Everything looks very chaotic. There are people, many unbelievably poor, who scrape by without any job. I wonder if I should really try to trade up here; the people here have other problems.

I enter the silk factory feeling uneasy. Inside, about twenty women perform various silk production tasks in terrible heat and poor light. It is very clear that this is no place for labor unions, thirty-five-hour work weeks, or employee representation. The women simply do what the grumpy boss commands. The boss knows why I am here, since his buddy wants to make the silk trade with me, and because of this, I have free access to the factory.

As a future owner of silk, I decide to do some work so that I can understand a bit about the production of it and I am handed a bucket of silkworm cocoons. The cocoons are about three-quarters of an inch long and are made of a soft, white fluff that is actually a single silk thread up to two thousand (!) feet long. Inside the cocoons are the worms, which have to be killed in a hot cooking pot, so I stand in front of a hot pot and dunk the cocoons into the water. But something goes wrong. The foreman is not very pleased when I take the cocoons out of the water and dunk them again. Everything sticks together until I just have a sticky white mass in my hands—the result is definitely not sup-posed to look like that. The women stand shyly in the back and laugh nervously behind their hands as I manage to screw everything up more than anyone else ever has.

The next step involves winding the silk threads onto a spool with the help of a spinning wheel called a swift. To this end, the worker casts the cocoon onto the swift in a specific manner, so that it catches the end of the silk thread and can roll it up. Managing it is a lot harder than it sounds for many reasons, and I have a hard time with it. To be honest, it is completely impossible for me. I try ten, twenty, thirty times before I give up, red in the face, and the twenty women take up again with giggles and whispers. I bow out of silk production permanently and just watch as the silk threads are turned into silk fabric on big looms.

I now finally meet the silk manufacturer, Ravi, who is friends with Kalian, Wiebke's colleague, and wants to trade silk for my tuk-tuk. He is dressed neatly compared to the foreman, seems very congenial, and greets me politely.

"Aha, you are the guy who wants to have the silk!" he says in greeting.

A knot in my chest unclenches. The communication with the travel agent Raj really worked—he had transferred the money for the silk and Ravi is willing to give me the promised silk. First, we make some small talk to warm up to each other. As much as I would like to get to the point, I have to be patient. Luckily, we soon turn to the theme of bartering. Ravi tells me that sixty years ago, shortly before the revolution under Gandhi, monetary transactions were discontinued and so silk was no longer sold, but rather, traded. There were unexpected benefits: suddenly anyone could barter using silk, regardless of the caste he belonged to. Ravi explains that after that era, the sale of silk was again caste-based, meaning silk could only be sold within a person's class. It's impressive what a positive effect bartering can have on human relations!

Now I'm just waiting for that effect to happen between Ravi and me. *Ravi, come on, let's get to the point already, dammit,* I think. Finally, he proudly shows me two saris that are meant to be worn by brides.

I smile and agree that they are very beautiful with their sequins and embroidery, until I realize that they are his trade offer. I react with reservation—I probably won't be able to trade Indian wedding dresses in Australia, my next leg!

I politely explain the situation to Ravi and request raw silk in exchange for the tuk-tuk. Luckily, Ravi understands the problem and he returns shortly with 240 feet of allegedly the finest silk in India in six different colors. Each forty-foot-long piece is folded into a manageable parcel so that I can carry all of the material in a cardboard box. I can't really say with certainty that this silk trade was a success, since I can't judge the quality of the silk as a layman, but Ravi seems to make a respectable enough. I think I have a good chance of trading the fabric in Australia; I researched online beforehand and found that the market value of silk is about four to six times higher in Australia than in India. If I do manage to trade the silk there, it will be a big step in the right direction.

Our Luxury Junk in the Slums

Before I can put my silk on the Australian bartering market, I spend another week in Mumbai, a metropolis of fourteen million people. The drive from the airport is hard to stomach because of the view: endless slums of tin shacks in rows and people begging everywhere. After the poverty in Bangalore, I hadn't envisioned something worse, but what Mumbai has to offer is simply shocking. The next few days I am sick in bed, probably from bacteria that found its way into my food. Maybe the images of poverty increased my susceptibility. I hardly have the energy to get to the door and I long for the flight to Australia, but I also ask around about who out of the fourteen million people in Mumbai knows something about bartering. The answers all point to the same place: the slum. Fifty-five percent of the residents of this city (almost eight million people) live in slums, and bartering seems to be ubiquitous there.

So I visit Dharavi, the largest slum in Asia, where a million people live in an area of less than one square mile. The conditions here, as expected, are disastrous. Poverty, tin shacks, narrow streets where power lines hang down to five feet above the ground, stinking sewers—and people everywhere who greet me with exceptional friendliness! Children and adults alike come up to me and absolutely have to take a picture with me. Wow, what an unexpected reception from people who know that I'm many times richer than them.

I later meet Chandarei, an older woman who carries a large tray of pots and plastic bowls on her head. She tells me that every day for forty years she has traded bowls and plates for second-hand clothing, which she then sells for a profit. Her method reminds me of Simon, the bartering pro from Cologne who works in a similar way, except among German companies instead of in a slum. It is interesting that Simon and Chandarei are so different, but their method of bartering is so similar. They both barter and then sell their results to a niche market for profit. I watch how Chandarei goes from shack to shack pitching her plates and bowls and then trades them for old clothes with people who are interested. During this process, she always looks dissatisfied. Her fellow worker tells me that that's a part of bartering—always keeping a poker face and acting displeased until you get the best deal you can get. I can hardly believe how callously and professionally business is conducted in the slum. I rejoiced so naively at every trade; it's no wonder my goods lost more and more value until I had just ten pounds of tea. I was too straightforward.

I continue on through the slum with my new knowledge of bartering, and head to so-called "Trash Street," a totally surreal place. A huge pipeline runs through the slum above ground, but it can hardly be seen under the three-foot pile of garbage around it, where several people live. Little children rummage through it, unphased by the dead dogs and sewers. I accidentally walk into a sewer in my open shoes and get scared that I'll be infected with some sort of disease.

Then I find myself in an area distinguished by huge piles of recyclable junk. Everywhere are mountains of old computers, children's toys, empty yogurt cups, and other plastic items that we in the

West have thrown away. Here, all of our luxury junk is separated and sorted according to size and material to be incinerated and turned into small plastic balls, which are then used to create new plastic products.

People with soot on their faces walk by me with huge bags of plastic junk. I go into the recycling building and watch men break old TVs with hammers under the dim fluorescent lights. It's so loud that my ears hurt. I talk to them and ask what exactly they do there. They tell me that the trash is sent from Europe and the US, and that they work for twenty-five euro cents per hour. I look in one of the bags and find children's toys from Germany that could have been in my own room twenty-five years ago. The space station and the telescope are not in there, but I recognize many of the other little figures. They certainly never imagined that after a happy time in a German child's room they would find their end like this, in a Dharavi slum. I wonder if the disposal of our luxury trash in India is a fair trade between Europe and India. It does create jobs in India, but it leaves a bad taste in your mouth to see our trash disposed of in the backyard of the third world—and how the people literally live *in* our waste.

I leave Dharavi depressed. I have never seen a place so burdened with problems anywhere else in the world. And yet among all this hardship, I have only met friendly people.

I have spent thirty-three days in India, during which I bartered four times. My little trip around Europe is completely overshadowed by India in terms of effort. I realize that I physically can't continue to endure this kind of exertion. I've had unexplained back pain for two weeks and diarrhea for days. I'm drinking liters of water, but I can't overcome that strain so quickly. The heat, the crowds, the cultural differences, the unfamiliar food, and the long days searching for people to barter with have knocked me out. I passed my limits and I know that I have to change my strategy. The idea of trading for a tuk-tuk at any cost was simply too exhausting. In the future, instead of searching first and foremost for bartering partners in a new place, I will rely more on my local contacts. After all, I have already traveled to almost seventy countries and built a Facebook "friend list" that recently passed the five-hundred mark. Friends can help when you are in a crisis. Why couldn't they also help me out in this situation?

5

PARASITE EXCHANGE

Australia

I'm in Perth—finally! The flight to Australia felt really good, not only because I have 240 feet of silk with me after my last successful trade, but also because I promise myself more straightforwardness and rationality in this western country. It should not only help me to successfully survive the rest of my bartering blitz, but also to get a handle on the physical exhaustion that I've developed in the past two weeks. After a visit to a doctor in Mumbai and a brief hospital stay due to my blood-pressure levels, no reason could be found for my serious case of diarrhea. So, now I place my hopes in this west Australian city.

After taking my daily antibiotic, I take a walk through the neighborhood. I can hardly enjoy its imposing, glassy skyline because at least once an hour I have to dash through the streets, annoying and embarrassing passersby with my exclamation: "bathroom, bathroom, bathroom!" This was also the case in the silk factory and during the two days in Dharavi: I talked to people and tried to barter, and then whoops—I'd have to run to the next toilet. My condition has begun to worry me more and more; I feel terribly tired, dizzy, and downtrodden. I worry that I picked up some kind of worm that is now slowly devouring my organs, relishing the decision of where to take a bite next. I've heard travel stories like this often and I have to laugh at my own wild imagination even as I visit the emergency room at a Perth hospital. Am I being paranoid? Unfortunately not. The doctor discovers that I picked up parasites in India that can only be removed from my intestines with a special mixture of medications. The doctor warns me that I'm making an uncomfortable trade: parasites for side-effects. I'm always looking ahead and I'm not afraid of uncertain trades, so I agree and pop all four tablets. After four days of emotional turmoil, it's all over. The parasites have accepted the trade and are hopefully gone forever.

I can finally devote myself to the silk and present my wonderful trade item to my first Australian. But most of the passersby on the streets of Perth wave me off. They don't seem to spontaneously know what to do with 240 feet of raw silk. That's why I film a little commercial.

"Silk Is Happiness!"

I lay out the forty-foot-long, six-foot-wide pieces of silk end to end in a gymnasium in the city, creating a colorful stretch of fabrics. I sprint along next to it in a sporty outfit and check my time: 8.7 seconds for 240 feet, almost as fast as when I was in the third grade. . . .

Later, in a city park, I wrap the silk around my neck and wear a two-foot-thick scarf. The Australians are amused by this larger than life, extremely eccentric scarf.

Then I drape the silk sheets over two park benches so that I can play underneath them like in a tent. I hear the passersby whispering about the increasing homelessness in Perth.

After that, it's time for the sack race. I convince a young Australian woman to wrap the silk around herself like I have, and then hop down seventy feet in a race. Neither of us can move our legs with the silk wrapped tightly around them. I fall over after just ten feet and see the woman standing at the finish line, smiling.

And you can play tug-o-war with the silk, too! I roll it together into one super rope and start a game, which the high-quality silk easily endures.

One morning, I realize what silk is really good for in Australia. I'm driving from Perth up the western coast in my rental car to visit a so-called Prince Leonard when I hear a terrifying message on the radio:

"Two out of three Australians develop skin cancer in their lifetime!"

I'm shocked that the ozone hole that has been over Australia for years has had such devastating consequences. I take the silk and cover the car windows so that I can drive the next 375 miles without the sun shining in.

A Whole Country, Not Just One House

I drive north because I've heard of Prince Leonard and could hardly believe it: years ago, in northwestern Australia, he founded his own country on a piece of land as big as Hong Kong. No joke! He just had enough of Australian politics one day, so he put up signs along the perimeter of his huge piece of land saying "Border" and "You are now entering the country of Hutt River." I had to see this with my own eyes. Someone like that must be eccentric and noble enough to be willing to barter for fine silk.

As I pass the "country borders," a border marker greets me. A little bit later, there stands an older man dressed in a crimson cloak. He is in front of a structure labeled "government building." As I get out of my car, he looks into the backseat and shakes his head at the big pile of silk completely wadded up into a ball. I won't be able to get rid of the silk like that, the prince makes clear. Before we chat more about trading, he invites me into the government building of Hutt River, the inside of which looks like an Australian farm inhabited by a mess of blow flies. There, he shows me all the proof that his state is real. He gives me various coins and bills that are in circulation in his country. They are very professionally made and say "Hutt River Dollar." In the small shop across from the government building, which is decorated with the national flag, I meet the princess of the state.

The eighty-year-old wife of the prince takes a two-dollar Hutt River coin and hands me a soda. As she processes the transaction, she shares how the life of a princess can be demanding. A life as a farmer's wife on a farm would definitely be easier, but still, she wouldn't trade her life as a princess for any other job.

Back in the government building, the prince stamps my passport officially and leads me past his white Rolls Royce (decorated with small Hutt River flags) to the parliament building. Five chairs stand around a cluttered table in a garage-like building. Prince Leonard sits at the head and motions for me to take a seat at the parliamentary table. He tells me that he considers trade between nations to be very important, which is why there are consulates representing Hutt River in various countries. I can vouch for that myself. A certain Mr. Slatow is the one who put me in contact with the prince, and he ran the "Hutt River Consulate in Germany" for several years.

However, trade between Hutt River and its closest neighbor apparently isn't going so well. The Australian government has long since had enough of the prince's secession attempt and has asked him to desist.

Prince Leonard describes how he officially declared war on Australia and rejected all Australian demands with his five-man (!) army. I stand across from the prince, look him in the eyes, and hardly know how to contain my laughter. This story is completely crazy.

The prince and I look at each other in silence for a few moments while I wait for a laugh from him to clarify that the war story is a joke. At the same time, he is waiting for my reaction, and presumably, a respectful one. When I don't arrive at one, an uncomfortable silence grows. I finally ask if such a military confrontation between countries is a smart idea. The prince says that that there are many things that just have to happen if you want to reach your goals.

At the end of my visit, he sees me to the border and we stand there surrounded by white desert. On one side, I'm in Australia, and on the other, the Kingdom of Hutt River. I ask if he is willing to set foot on Australian ground in farewell, but apparently that is too much exchange with the neighboring enemy. I still offer him a symbol of exchange with Germany, a Bavarian beer stein. He trades it for a Hutt River flag, which he hands to its new owner over the border to Australia.

As I set off on my way, I see the prince in my rearview mirror for a while, standing alone and a little bit lost at his border marker. I wonder how he benefits in any way from founding his bizarre country. Doesn't he ever want to go down to the local Australian pub for a drink? Life is much easier when you dedicate yourself to bartering and not to seceding!

I drive back to Perth with the image of the sad prince in my head. At the same time I think that if a farmer somewhere in Australia can found his own state, I will certainly be able to make it to a house in Hawaii, right?

On the 375-mile stretch between Hutt River and Perth, there is nothing: no people, no phone reception, no Internet. It is crazy to me that after visiting overcrowded India, I am in a country about as big as Europe but with a population only somewhat larger than the state of New York. Luckily, there is a small village with a gas station at the midpoint. I end up knocking on a door in the early evening to ask about lodging. A corpulent lady over the age of sixty named Betty opens the door and invites me in. She is excited to have an unexpected visitor. In her remote location, she doesn't have much interaction with other people and invites me to spend the night. She tells me that the sparse population is a real problem in cases of illness, since the nearest hospital is hours away. If you have a heart attack, you'll be gone halfway to the hospital! She laughs, then becomes serious again and continues that this is the reason why she is moving in with her daughter in the next town next month. In this area there is also no trade activity, since to trade you do need other people. So I quickly head back to Perth.

My experience with the dissenting prince in the unpopulated area has made me think. I decide to start a little campaign in Perth to promote friendly trade between people in general, and between Australia and Hutt River in particular. To these ends, I retrieve a friend's gift from my backpack: the love blanket. It is a pretty, snuggly wool blanket with a big red heart that you can cuddle with until nothing but your face is sticking out. If that's not a symbol for the exchange of warmth and love, I don't know what is!

I make my way to the pedestrian mall in Perth with it. I go up to passersby, hug them earnestly, and explain that I'm an ambassador from Hutt River sent to improve trade relations between the countries. Surprisingly, they have all heard of Hutt River and Prince Leonard, so many accept my hugs. The passersby laugh and ask me to end this devastating war and to let freedom come to Hutt River. I spend a day exchanging symbolic love and warmth with the residents of Perth, especially with many young and attractive women. There's freedom in the land again!

Crocodile Wigge

The next day I call Mr. Slatow in Berlin, the "ambassador" who had told me about Hutt River and the prince. I thank him for the interesting contact, but tell him that I haven't been able to get rid of the crumpled silk, explaining that I have a deadline and that I was put in contact with Jim Rogers, a billionaire in Singapore, through an American friend. He would like to make a trade with me in the next two weeks—but only if I have jade to barter. Slatow combs his brain for someone who could offer me some jade immediately, and advises me to go to an Australia expat in the Northern Territory who has run the travel agency Travel North for decades.

A day later, I am in an airplane to Darwin to meet Werner Sarny. My silk is all neatly rolled up again. Werner is over seventy, has a large frame, looks a little like Indiana Jones, and is ready to barter—as long as he can have some fun! Fine then . . . I ask him how I can help with that. "A test of courage!" he says with a grin.

"A test of courage? What kind of test?"

"It has to do with crocodiles and snakes," he answers without blinking.

"Are you serious?"

"Yeah, it'll be fun, you'll see. And if you can do it, we'll trade."

Werner owns many camping and RV sites in the Northern Territory and has made more than enough money in his life. Now, he just likes to have fun. I don't really understand how this barter is going to pan out, but I go along with it since I have to trade. And somehow I also find it entertaining to try out something different. So why not a quirky test of courage?

The next day, I am standing in the Crocodile and Snake Center in Darwin, on the northern coast of Australia. This area is swarming with crocodiles; the movie *Crocodile Dundee* was filmed here.

For my first test, I have to tease three-year-old crocodiles with a bit of meat on a fishing pole. The crocodile teens snap wildly, but there's no real danger from where I stand behind the protection of a three-foot Plexiglas wall.

My second test is to feed a dead rat to a giant python. This time, I'm really scared. I stretch my hand toward the hissing snake when it strikes with unbelievable force and I fall backwards out of fear. The workers at the center are standing next to me, keeping a watchful eye on the snake to make sure that Crocodile Wigge doesn't suddenly disappear down its throat.

After pulling myself together, I get to hold a baby crocodile on my arm. It's only twelve inches long, but it can already bite down and latch on. It's somehow adorable, but I can't pet it like a puppy since we never really warm up to each other.

For my fourth test, they drape the giant python around my neck. It's very heavy and I can feel its muscles as it coils around my neck and torso. For a while, I can actually hold back my fear, but when it looks directly in my eyes with its flickering tongue, I lose it. There is simply too little space between my own head and the snake's. The snake handler next to me recognizes my paralyzed stare and quickly removes the monster.

Test five is very exciting but unforgettably traumatizing: they put me in a crocodile tank in the "Cage of Death," a six-foot Plexiglas cage, so that I can stare through my goggles into the 127-toothed jaw of a sixteen-foot crocodile named Hector. He finds my presence in his territory to be pretty uncool. Funnily enough, there are approximately one-inch gaps built into the Plexiglas cage, so that I could, theoretically, make physical contact with Hector (which would be the end of my trip). He and I look at each other for about an eighth of a second before I try to beg his forgiveness with a hand gesture. This sign of regret doesn't work. Hector bites at the cage with all his fury. I scramble through the (completely secure) cage in terror and manage to throw my back out so that for the next weeks, I can only walk hunched over (for real). After this torture, I am sure that I have earned a high class jade/silk trade with Werner Sarny. The five tests of courage have pushed me to my limits.

The next day, I drive past Kakadu National Park towards Katherine, the only town in a radius of over six hundred miles from Darwin. Again I drive through endless scrubland with no humans in sight. Werner later tells me that there are only eighteen thousand people here, in an area the size of Germany. It's unbelievable how empty it is. It becomes clear that if Werner Sarny is not interested in bartering, I will hardly be able to find anyone else—I'm totally dependent on him. I indicate the urgency of this trade and he patiently inspects the silk.

"Yes, I like it!" he finally says. I'm so relieved! "But I see everything up until now as training. You could do one more little test!" The older gentleman in his Crocodile Dundee outfit smiles at me. I can't believe it! My video project for Panta in India at least had a real purpose; with Werner, it's just about amusing him. With so few people in the area, this is perhaps somewhat understandable. Werner has an amused but very congenial energy, so I agree to the next test with a chuckle.

We ride along the Katherine River toward the sunset in his boat. Nature overflows into the river, mosquitoes bite, and crickets chirp cheerfully in the tropical climate. Oh yeah, and now and then, curious crocodiles poke their heads out of the water.

"Michael, are you excited yet? They're actually quite sweet!"

Werner laughs, particularly when he notices how terrified I look. He gives me a friendly whop on the back.

"Come on, you'll find this fun."

Well, maybe later, but at this moment there's no hint of fun. We get out on a little beach and Werner shines his flashlight on a ten-foot crocodile lying on the beach with its snout sticking out of the water. He laughs and lovingly calls it "Mousie."

"Isn't it sweet? Little Mousie," I hear him say. I can't really share his good humor about the situation. He gives me a few pieces of meat for crocodile food. I slowly approach the crocodile with my arm stretched out while Werner looks on in amusement.

"Michael, come on, you can get a little closer. Or are you already wetting your pants?"

Mousie hardly moves as I approach, and it feels like the calm before the storm. After all, just today I made some videos of another river crocodile as it suddenly jumped up to scare me with its jaws gaping. In slow motion, the video looks like a clip from *Godzilla*, *Jurassic Park*, or *Texas Chainsaw Massacre*, if the chainsaw was made of 127 crocodile teeth. I know that despite Werner's experience, I have to be very careful with this test of courage. It can all go south really fast. I think of the famous animal show star, Steve Irwin, who held his head between those 127 teeth in a risky on-camera experiment. His program apparently had up to five hundred million viewers worldwide, including many in Germany. It was all good fun until it suddenly went bad and he was stabbed in the stomach by a sting ray . . . and he was gone. Considering this, I insist on feeding only a slightly more predictable freshwater crocodile and not a saltwater crocodile like Hector.

So I approach Mousie slowly as it looks at me patiently. I creep up with the meat in my hand.

Thirteen feet—Mousie looks calm. Eight feet—Mousie is still looking at me peacefully. In the background, Werner calls out, "Come on Michael, get closer!" I get scared and can't help but think of Steve Irwin, whose success made him careless. No, I don't want to meet my end like that, no way. But then Werner calls out again, "Michael, let's go, Mousie is waiting!" I dare to get a little closer, my knees shaking, until I'm less than two feet away. I fling the hunk of meat down on the beach and dash away. If the crocodile had popped up, my two feet of distance would have been much too little. But luckily the animal doesn't need to display its true power when a hunk of meat is lying on the beach. The meat disappears before I can blink, and Mousie disappears into the river faster than I can believe. My heart has practically stopped—Werner's too, from laughing. Werner throws his arm around me and confesses that Mousie has seen many tourists and is very predictable. He continues to laugh, but after my adrenaline crashes, I'm just worn out.

Then things become more relaxed. I spend a few more lovely hours under an intensely starry sky that can't be seen in Europe because of the light pollution. Werner and I grill steaks and drink red wine. He grins and reassures me that he knew nothing could happen to me during the six tests of courage.

The next morning, I meet Werner on his farm in the Katherine Gorge, a heavenly canyon where the high yellow desert rock looks like something from an Old Western film set. Werner is waiting for me in his crocodile hunter getup, already grinning.

"So, how did you sleep?" he asks immediately.

"Yeah, yeah. I dreamed about crocodiles, of course."

"Then I have the perfect thing for you to remember our little games!"

Werner takes my big roll of silk and puts a white roll of about the same size, but lighter, in my hand. I am supposed to open it. I roll out an over six-foot long painting on a table in front of the farm. It is by the Aborigine painter Barra Barra, who is internationally famous from his exhibitions in London and Germany. Three big crocodiles are painted in earth tones in the picture. Unbelievable! The painting is beautiful and it is clear that I made a very profitable trade. In a brochure about the painting, there's a four-figure appraisal of the current market value, in dollars. Wow, the jump from India to Australia and the six crocodile tests really paid off. After fewer than two months of bartering, I seem to be in good shape. The difficult weeks in India are forgotten and the tension of the past few days falls away. Werner and I are both happy.

As I leave, I see Werner's wife Patricia trying out the silk as a tablecloth. Why not? It's an option I hadn't thought of. . . .

Lost in the Western World

As happy as I am to have this painting, the billionaire Jim Rogers is expecting me in Singapore in six days, and I promised him jade. I know turning the painting into a precious stone is a very difficult task. I give it a shot with the Aborigines, the native inhabitants of Australia in the Northern Territory. Maybe they will be excited about a painting by their famous artist and also happen to have a few jade stones lying around. But it becomes apparent that I shouldn't just drive into their villages. Locals react with irritation to my request to visit the Aborigines. I quickly realize that the native people are a taboo topic and that relations between Australians and Aborigines are not so great. On the streets I see many Aborigines walking around in broad daylight with big bottles of beer. Others sit strung out on park benches or in front of buildings.

Instead of speaking directly to the Aborigines, I meet with Petranny, an Australian woman who displays Aboriginal art in a gallery and employs some as artists. Manuel, a dark-skinned man with a white beard in his mid-forties, is one of them. He paints in a style similar to Barra Barra. He and Petranny tell me that relations between Australians and Aborigines have improved, but integration just isn't happening—their mentalities are too different. While Australians, like Europeans and Americans, believe in being efficient, pragmatic, and rational, Aborigines live in nature and practice their religion, which most Australians think of as superstition. So it's not very shocking that the government's social aid programs often miss their intended audience, as many Aborigines are not as invested in money as The Man would like.

Petranny says that she gives Aborigines like Manuel work in her gallery to help keep them off the streets and away from alcohol, but she also says that she is often exasperated. She explains that she expects a western work style from her employees, such as compliance with tax deadlines and predictable productivity, but that she is regularly disappointed in that area.

Manuel offers to teach me a bit more about the traditions of the Aborigines. First, he teaches me to play a didgeridoo. It's sounds like ridiculous honking until I learn to blow the air through my lips to create the correct tone. Then he shows me how to make a fire with two pieces of wood and some straw. I rub one stick up and down the other, and rub and rub until my arms are falling off. Manuel encourages me to continue, until I can hardly feel my arms anymore. But with a bit of help from him, a spark appears between the sticks. A little later, after one last high speed rub, one of the sticks catches fire. I lay it in the hay and blow on it until it's burning away!

Then, Manuel shows me how to throw an Aboriginal wooden spear with a boomerang attached at one end. On my first try, I throw the boomerang and it just falls to the ground. Manuel laughs himself silly. Then I study the design: I use the boomerang as a stabilizer and support for the spear, and hold on to it after the throw, so that it hits a cardboard kangaroo with full power and goes right through it. Manuel is impressed. He says that this has been a successful trade between a German and Aborigine. I get the impression that Manuel wishes that Australians were more interested in Aboriginal culture—understanding between cultures might be better then.

Since Manuel and Petranny have no use for the painting, I go online and put out a call for help on my Facebook and travel blog: "Who knows a jade dealer who would be interested in a spontaneous trade with me? Please, please, I'll do anything!"

In the next two days I get a lot of replies, mostly with the advice that I should fly to New Zealand. The Maori, the native people there, are jade experts and the country is an excellent place for jade due to its location on the ring of fire, the fault line around the Pacific.

To pass the time before I leave Australia, I go to a hippie market in Darwin, where I meet a card reader. He sits behind a table and lays down cards with images of skulls, dark clouds, and mystical symbols. I wonder if he can give me as much encouragement for my trip as the psychic in Germany. He turns various cards over, all while looking very serious. On one is a skeleton. Just as I consider leaving, he gives me a few concrete words of advice, without knowing anything about the bartering experiment.

"Plan better in the coming months or you will not reach your goal!"

"Don't just concentrate on the end goal. The journey is the reward."

"You will do everything you want, but not in the time you want to!"

"You will reach your goal, but not the way you expect. I see money!"

What did he say? He sees money? If I managed to get $500,000 for something in Hawaii, which I could use to buy a house, that wouldn't be bad. I don't get an exact image of the future from his words, but even so, I take the advice. It's better to plan and to enjoy the journey.

6

HELP AT THE END OF THE WORLD

New Zealand

After my little bartering weather forecast, I realize that I have just one hundred hours left to meet Jim Rogers in Singapore for a Jade trade. Since I don't get any more tips from the Internet, I just get on a plane. A day later, I'm standing in front of high-rise façades in Auckland that could have come from the US. I roll out my crocodile painting on the curb and ask people as they pass by if they want to trade it for some jade, but New Zealanders don't seem to be so spontaneous.

A bit later, I see Maori protesters with big banners reading "No oil drilling on our land!" and "Leave us in peace!" It doesn't seem to be utopia between the settlers and the native inhabitants. I scramble inconspicuously through the crowd with my crocodile painting. Just like at the antinuclear power protest in Cologne, I shout along with the crowd's chanting: "End oil drilling on our land!"

Many Maori look at me in confusion: a white man shouting to white people to get off his land that doesn't even belong to him. But many are also amused by the presence of this unusual guest and pat me appreciatively on the back. At some point I ask a young Maori protester if he knows where I can barter for jade. At first he doesn't understand the question, since his thoughts are completely on oil drilling, but then he has a hot tip: "Go to the village of Rotorua, where the biggest Maori population is!"

I follow his advice and head there. On the way, I struggle through sheep fields with the big painting, which I've draped over my shoulders like a cape. As far as I can see, New Zealand is mostly composed of big, bright green, hilly grasslands. A wonderful and relaxing view—if these fields weren't full of bleating sheep. As far as the eye can see: sheep! They stare at me and the crocodile painting, then run away, bleating wildly. Apparently they don't like crocodiles. I feel like a shepherd among thousands of sheep that all have to be led home. But I actually just want to barter, and I'm relieved when I get to the Maori village.

I'm greeted by hot springs with giant billowing sulfur clouds, the ones you see in photos of exotic islands. It's obvious that the Maori village is on a volcano. In front of the village meeting house, I meet Te Rangintirio Rekawaway Te Moanaoaoaku. Now that's what I call a name. My name, on the other hand, doesn't knock Te Rangintirio Rekawaway Te Moanaoaoaku's socks off.

"Oh, another white guy named Michael!"

Te Rangintirio Rekawaway Te Moanaoaoaku is in his late thirties, has brown skin, and wears a lumberjack shirt and dark sunglasses. He tells me that he lived in Australia for almost twenty years, but after the deaths of his parents he had to come back to the Maori and fulfill his duties as head of the family. He tells me that in New Zealand, the cultural differences between the native residents and the settlers are big, but integration has worked better. He talks about a big land reform in the nineties, which gave the Maori back a lot of land that had been taken by European colonists.

He says that Maori children mostly go to school and that alcoholism is far less of a problem than among the Australian Aborigines. He also says that since these reforms, New Zealanders may no longer mine jade in the country, since the deposits are located on Maori land. I didn't know that! So I definitely have to go through the Maori if I want jade.

I get right to the point and spread out the painting on the ground in front of the mystical wooden face decorating the meeting house. Te Rangintirio Rekawaway Te Moanaoaoaku thinks it would be exciting to have something in the village from the native people of their neighboring island, but he can't fulfill my wish for a jade exchange.

"You have to understand that we only pass down jade within families from generation to generation. Even if I wanted to, I couldn't give you any jade!"

I can't process this. I went to New Zealand in total wide-eyed naivete. If I'd just done a little more research in advance, I wouldn't be sitting here depressed in front of the meeting house with Te Rangintirio

Rekawaway Te Moanaoaoaku. But then I wouldn't have met the man with the most interesting name I've ever heard.

Luckily, I have one more option. A friend told me on Facebook that she knows John & John from Jade Mountain, two jade artists from New Zealand, and that they agreed I could come by. Now there are less than three days before my flight to Jim Rogers in Singapore, one of the one thousand richest men on the planet. I stand in front of the jade grinding shop of John Senior and John Junior and watch through their big storefront as they use dental-looking drills to turn jade into art pieces and jewelry. Two other family members help them as well.

John & John seem pretty relaxed, like most New Zealanders. No wonder, when you live far from the rest of the world on two big islands, surrounded by fewer than five million people (and at least as many sheep), amidst the phenomenal nature. John & John show me their jade storage where there are tons of green stones, but they are all imported from China, since jade mining is no longer allowed here. I see a deep green, multi-pound stone of raw jade. I offer John Senior my hand to shake on the deal. He's totally taken off guard. He shakes my hand. "Good, the deal is done!" I say, laughing. John laughs along, but then he clarifies that things are not quite that simple. What a shame!

Together we inspect the crocodile painting in his workshop. I have good luck. John Senior collects art and is very interested in the painting. I explain the entire story about the house in Hawaii and how I'm meeting Jim Rogers in less than three days. John Senior understands my situation and offers me two jade items: a four-inch figurine and a Maori amulet to be worn on a chain. John mentions that the two jade pieces together have a four-figure value, but I'm hesitant. The two pieces are definitely beautiful, but could perhaps have no value at all. You hear about fake jade all the time (I've read up). I remember the woman from the Dharavi slum who gave me the tip to look dissatisfied to get the best deal, so I act disappointed in front of John & John, even though I don't really like performing this act.

John thinks about it after I argue that the painting is something really special and is an investment. And who wouldn't like to have crocodiles hanging in their living room? (Not me after all that croc-related stress.) John is convinced. He goes into the storage room and returns with the six-and-a-half-pound jade stone that I had wanted to abscond with a few hours ago. I'm done. The stone is approximately twelve by ten inches and deep green. I'm unendingly thankful; I'd never have bet on this deal.

My tears of happiness don't stop. John Junior joins us and offers to take me into the workshop so I can cut a little jade figurine myself. A short while later, I have my protective goggles, headphones, smock, and dental drill. With John's help, I shape a small jade stone into an approximately two-inch house. It's my long-desired Hawaiian dream home.

John & John explain that they are being so generous because they think my bartering journey is a good idea, but also because they live so far from the rest of the world. John Senior says that people with crazy projects rarely pop up in rural New Zealand. Wow, I would never have thought that New Zealand's isolation would have such a positive effect on my bartering blitz.

John Senior shares one more reason: the trading of jade has had an important part in New Zealand's history since the Maori sailed between the islands and traded jade for their livelihood. Sure, the jade now comes from Russia and China, but they still feel a duty to the tradition.

7

MY FIRST BILLIONAIRE BUDDY

Singapore

After sixty-five days of bartering, I sit with my jade on a plane, and I'm just in time. Jim Rogers, the billionaire in Singapore, promised me weeks ago to devote thirty minutes of his precious time to me on May 25th at exactly 11:10 a.m., just as long as I bring some jade with me. And I have it!

I call up the most important facts about Jim again:

He retired from finance at the age of thirty-seven, since he has made enough money in the stock market.

He moved from New York to Singapore as an adventurer and investor.

He is married to a young blonde.

He has made two big world-wide trips, one on a motorcycle, and in the process set a world record: over one hundred countries visited in three years!

Now I understand why I was granted an audience. Jim likes adventures. He has also written books about them with telling titles such as *Investment Biker* and *Adventure Capitalist*. I'm very excited for my appointment as I prepare myself. A meeting with a billionaire is *the* chance to really make a big jump. So I have devised the following plan: first, I'll offer only the two small jade pieces, and then I'll throw in the big stone, and then, when I've already gotten a decent offer, BAM! the little jade Hawaii house is also on the table. And then, when that has added a nice amount to his offer, Jim Rogers will turn the house over and, *ding!* the inscription "for Jim" on the bottom, which I wisely made in advance. Who could refuse an offer like that?

It is May 25, exactly 11:10 a.m., when I ring the bell to Jim's house, or should I say his estate, in Singapore. A maid leads me to a conference room decorated with Asian art objects. I wait ten minutes until an older but athletic man of just 5'4" enters the room, says hello, and gets right to the point: "Did you bring jade?"

"Yes!"

"Let's see it."

"Here, two beautiful jade art pieces."

"It doesn't really look like good jade."

"No, here are the certificates."

"They aren't real!"

Unbelievable! I was so sure that a totally euphoric bartering agreement would happen here, interrupted only by the clinking of champagne flutes and the entrance of attractive maids who would discreetly shove caviar hors d'oeuvres into my mouth.

And then this: a brutal business deal where I have to be extremely careful not to leave the house empty-handed. I realize that Jim will disparage anything I offer to strengthen his own position. But luckily, the image of the woman in the Dharavi slum of Mumbai appears before my eyes again. She whispers in my ear: "When bartering, always act as like you are completely dissatisfied!"

I immediately have the opportunity to put those words into action. Jim offers me two gold coins, an ounce each. When you think about the fact that an ounce of gold is worth about $1,500, that's not bad. But still, I listen to the words of the woman from the slum and act dissatisfied. At the same time, I set the six-and-a-half-pound jade stone—*bam!*—on the crystal table like magic. Jim looks at the jade with big eyes. He hadn't counted on there being more. Now the shell of the stony businessman is beginning to crumble, I think, as he says, "What is *that*?"

"Six and a half pounds of jade."

"It doesn't look like good jade."

"No, here's the certificate."

"Come on, it'll cost me $10,000 to get it cut."

I almost have a small crisis, but luckily Jim disappears wordlessly into his gold and silver cabinet and places a third ounce of gold on the table. Wow! That's almost $5,000 in gold, and I'll definitely be able to trade it, since gold has value all over the world, which makes it much better than jade. And the best thing is that I still have my trump card. The moment comes—*ding!*—I place the little house wordlessly on the table at the same moment Jim looks at the door politely but impatiently. My thirty-minute time with the billionaire is over.

"And what is *that* now?"

"A jade Hawaiian house that I made myself, for you."

I don't say anything, I don't show a certificate, I just calmly turn the house over. Then I say, in my most charming voice, "I made it especially for you. It has an inscription, here: *for Jim.*"

"An inscription? For me? That's . . ."

Both of us feel tears in our eyes. For a moment, emotions win over the tough business atmosphere. Jim disappears into his cabinet again. It takes a moment, but he returns with three ounces of silver, which he puts in my hand with a smile, but without wasting words. He quickly sees me to the door, probably so as not to risk me seeing him wipe the tears. Or maybe just so that I can't magically proffer another piece of jade out of my pocket.

Wow, I made a good deal and now I'm sitting with three ounces of gold and three ounces of silver in a hostel room in hot, humid Singapore, right on the equator. This city state is distinguished by its imposing skyline and its atmosphere of order and cleanliness that beats out Germany in every way. It's a great city, but with unusually strict laws. A taxi driver tells me that the slightest infringement is punished immediately with jail time. I wonder if I'm allowed to walk around Singapore with six ounces of gold and silver in my pocket. I hastily look for my next country and decide on Thailand.

8

THE GREAT TRADE-OUT

Thailand

With the gold and silver discreetly tucked away in my wallet, I walk through Patong in Phuket. Patong could be considered the Mallorca of Asia, with the small difference that the tsunami came through here a few years ago, and the city still hasn't completely recovered from it. Hundreds of massage girls stand on the side of the road, trying to pull one of the few Farangs (foreigners) into their booth. "Farang, Farang! Handsome man! Farang, come here, nice massage. Make you very happy!"

On the search for trade partners in Phuket, I realize that many of the massage girls are actually ladyboys: boys who have switched their gender through hormones, plastic surgery, and a bit of clever makeup. The trading of one's own gender might be the most fascinating topic of trade on my trip so far, especially since this trade seems so final. So I talk with two massage girls, Linda and Amy. They are both in their mid-twenties and look like pretty, young women. They tell me that there are many reasons for someone to decide to change their sex, and that many young men in Thailand are doing it.

Linda tells me that female hormones are very easy and cheap to buy in the pharmacy in Thailand, which is unthinkable in many countries, but ladyboys are surprisingly accepted. According to them, Thai culture pretty much treats ladyboys like any other women, even though they can't have many official jobs due to their gender mix. In the happy massage business with tourists, they can actually earn much more money than they could have as boys. Linda says that she easily earns two to three thousand baht in a day, which is about eighty dollars. That's more than many Thai workers earn in a month. So aside from the personal desire to be a woman, there is also a business aspect for the many boys changing their sex in Thailand.

Starting with an apple in Germany.

Attempting to balance fifty smoothies at an anti-nuclear
demonstration.

Crossing Germany on a dear friend, Herman.

With the tuk-tuk in India before being repaired and painted.

A desperate attempt to barter Indian silk in New Zealand.

With Prince Leonard in his kingdom of Hutt River.

Bartering raw meat in India—not the smartest idea in 100-degree heat.

Feeding a wild crocodile in Australia.

Climbing Mount Kilimanjaro wearing some lederhosen.

On top of Mount Kilimanjaro.

Racing against former Olympic champ, Paul Bitok, in Kenya.

Barter deal with Ukrainian pop star Ruslana in Kiev.

Trying out a new look at the Burning Man festival, and getting some BMX bikes as presents.

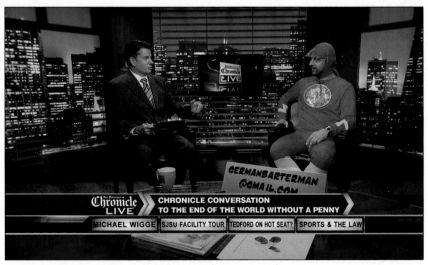

Barterman on *Chronicle Live* television show.

Barterman and Coati Mundi rapping in LA.

Final goal reached: A house in Hawaii after 200 days,
14 countries, and 42 barter deals!

As I am not looking to exchange my sex, I have to move on to find a way to get rid of my gold. It seems that Thailand is traded out. No one appears interested in gold and silver. A European who wants to barter gold in the streets is a bit too much for polite Thai people. It seems like a good time to move on.

9

AFRICA TILL YOU DROP

Tanzania

I still haven't been to Africa, and it's not too far away, but there are so many countries there and I need to figure out which one is best for trading. I don't want to make another faux pas like in Thailand.

I sit with the map of Africa and run my finger through the countries.

Libya, the Ivory Coast, and Sudan are out of the question due to their political conditions. Then there is South Africa and Tunisia, which I have already visited, and I would like to see new countries. In Mozambique and Angola, they speak Portuguese, which I don't know, and I don't know French, which rules out many West African countries. Then there are the western Saharan countries that the Dakar Rally went through for decades until they moved to South America out of fear of Islamic extremists. So I would rather stay away from there.

Some African countries stick out in my mind from the eighties and nineties charity ads with pictures of undernourished children, like beautiful Malawi or Ethiopia, which are some of the poorest in the world. Trading gold and silver there would be a step beyond scornful. Somalia is known for its dysfunctional government and for pirates who take over freight ships, and people there are definitely not interested in bartering. Then there's Zimbabwe, where President Mugabe initiated distaste for white visitors. So, maybe not there either.

I'm unsure. I look at the map of the huge continent. It might be the most beautiful, with fantastic nature reserves, rivers, mountains, animals, and surely an endless number of friendly people. And I don't know where I should head if I don't want to make a mistake. So I ask for help on my travel blog again:

HEY, WHERE SHOULD I GO IN AFRICA? HELP!

The decision is made two days later: East Africa! Tanzania and Kenya are both totally available to tourists, there is no current political unrest, and, I admit it, another one of my childhood dreams is to wave down from the peak of Kilimanjaro.

Eight hours later I get off the plane at the Kilimanjaro airport. The big, white mountain that was called "Kaiser Wilhelm Peak" when Tanzania was a part of "German East Africa" greets me from the runway with its imposing snow cap that disappears into the clouds. I feel like I am going to have a few exciting weeks here. I prepare for my next barter attempt in a hostel in Arusha. I prepare arguments for the upcoming barter in my usual manner. I think about what the gold and silver coins could be used for if you don't want to use them as money:

Gold coin as a sundial: place a cigarette on top of the coin and shine a flashlight on it.

Gold coin as a sink stopper: lay a coin in the drain opening. Unbelievably, gold coins are exactly the same size as regular sink drains!

Gold coin as a board game piece: in case you lose one of your board game pieces (for instance, on a long bartering trip).

Gold coin as drawing tool: trace around a gold coin with a pencil. If you want to paint a sun or the wheels of a car, you get a perfect circle.

Gold coin as stabilizer for a wobbly table: pile three coins on top of each other, place them under the short leg, and the table is steady again.

I go through Arusha to get a feel for potential gold trading in Africa with my coins sewed to the inside of my jacket in a transparent sleeve for security. At a car repair shop, twenty African men immediately gather around to see the three shiny gold coins inside my jacket. There is a lot of curiosity for that much sparkle, until someone expresses doubt. "I don't believe a word. Those coins are not real!"

I reply that they are real gold and that I want to trade them for something else. The group laughs and one points at me. I'm exposed as a white conman, and despite high-fives and laughter, I can no longer prove my trustworthiness here. A bit later, I meet Onzen by the side of the road. He looks like the shady, disreputable salesman on the corner that you are *not* supposed to trust. A five-inch scar over his left cheek confirms this. Disreputable meets disreputable, I think, something could happen here!

I cautiously show him the three gold coins in my jacket and offer to trade. Onzen is interested and shows me two gemstones, tanzanite, which sparkles in blue and pink. I really like them. I have read about these gems in travel guides. They have only been mined in Tanzania since the sixties and can have double the value in Western countries than in Tanzania. I'm curious, but Onzen just repeats: "Money, money, give me money for them!"

The day passes like that with more nos. I meet some children with a bicycle who wouldn't trade it for $5,000 in gold, and a group of young men who won't even trade their sneakers for it. The explanation is always the same: first, they see me as a potential conman who wants to pawn off fakes, and second, they don't like to trade because they need money. I decide to give up on offering the gold in the street, since I don't want to step on any toes.

My taxi driver, Baraka, explains the situation. The people in Tanzania don't like to barter, since money has a much higher value to them than some random goods. How does an object help them in their everyday struggle to survive when they can't use it to buy dinner? The country is among the thirty poorest countries in the world. The monthly income per person is approximately 130 dollars, and every third citizen lives below the poverty line. It's beyond inappropriate to try to barter gold here. Baraka advises me to travel to Kenya, which might be better—they have a flourishing tourist industry with wealthy visitors.

I notice that something in me bristles at accepting my mistakes. I don't want to give up so quickly and move on to another country again. If I really do have to cross the borders again, I want to at least face a new challenge—I don't want to make it too easy for myself.

It's Kilimanjaro that calls to me. Between the city of Arusha, where I am now, and Kenya, fifty miles away, stands Kilimanjaro, Africa's highest mountain. Traveling over this mountain to get to Kenya would be a crazy and unforgettable adventure (which, as I said, is also one of those childhood dreams I immersed myself in with my school atlas).

Furthermore, it would save me the risk of running into customs problems at the Kenyan border if they were to find my gold and silver coins. The path over Kilimanjaro would be easier at least in that way. You take the Umbwe route for an unbelievable 19,300 feet, and then from the summit you take the old smuggler's path down the other side and go through the Rongai route, which leads directly to Kenya—bypassing the troublesome customs.

I already have the jitters thinking that the few days of training I did in a local gym won't be enough for this physical feat. Crossing over the highest mountain in Africa isn't child's play. At 19,300 feet, it is always snow capped, even right on the equator, and easily dwarfs the highest mountain in Europe, the 15,700-foot-high Mont Blanc.

I think it would be a fun farewell for the locals to watch the crazy German during his preparatory training. So, I start training for the crossing in Arusha's busy fruit market in my sweat band and gym clothes. There are no stands at the market; the sellers offer their wares out of baskets that they carry easily on their heads. The market is frantic as I calmly begin my training program: sit-ups, push-ups, tricep exercise, and a bit of jogging—these are the basic exercises that cause grins among the African fruit sellers and customers. It's not every day that the only white person around does foolish exercises on the muddy street. But when I start my mango-weight lifting (seventeen mangoes in a basket), the market visitors can hardly contain their laughter. They cheer me on from all sides. I explain to someone who asks that I'm preparing for an important mission: crossing Kilimanjaro. The mistrust that many people seemed to have for me before is forgotten when it becomes obvious that this white guy has a good, self-deprecating sense of humor. I spend a very sporty afternoon in the fruit market gaining that last little bit of fitness I need for my big Kilimanjaro crossing.

Kaiser Wilhelm Peak, It Hurts!

And then it's time! Among my repertoire of typical German items that I brought for the purpose of cultural exchange (the beer stein found a good home in Hutt River), I also have a hiking outfit, and it's finally time to bring it out.

As I start out on my way to climb Kilimanjaro, I wear lederhosen, a checkered shirt, red knee socks, and a Bavarian mountain hat. The African porter Eric laughs out loud at my appearance.

"You look like one of the Germans who came here 130 years ago."

Oh geez, I really hadn't thought about that, especially since I'm not trying to glorify colonial history, but rather promote cultural exchange. I quickly become enmeshed in a long-winded explanation of why I'm dressed like this. Luckily, Eric doesn't seem to take offense at my outfit. We have very good conversation as we hike 6,500 feet through the rainforest. Eric carries a fifty-five-pound bag on his head that he won't let me relieve him of. He tells me that he knows a lot about the colonial history and knows what Kilimanjaro used to be called and that the summit was climbed for the first time in the late nineteenth century by a German named Hans Meyer.

When I ask what he thinks of the colonial time under the Germans, Eric surprises me by saying that exchange with the Germans brought a lot of positive things to Tanzania, such as better infrastructure and an extensive rail system. Then he says that there was also an exchange of words between languages. In Swahili, they use the word "Schule" for school and carrots are "Karotti." But an exchange would not be an exchange if the other side had not received something too. For example, Germans use the word "safari," which comes from Swahili and there simply means "trip."

Eric and I march up the mountain through the humid, warm rainforest and talk animatedly the whole time. Eric tells me that he gets about ten euros for six days, which I find shockingly low after having paid the tour company one thousand euro. He tells me that he would really like to study law, but it costs a prohibitive $800 per year. So he sees his future on the mountain—up with fifty-five pounds, down with fifty-five pounds, and up again with fifty-five pounds!

It shocks me to see in the moment that I am also a part of this structure if I make use of Eric's services. I start to ponder how I could support Eric, but I don't find an answer at this point. To relax the mood a little, I pull out the golden hunting horn that completes my hiking outfit, but which also makes a good hiding place for my gold and silver coins so I can bring them into Kenya inconspicuously via the smugglers' route. I have already hidden them in the mouth of the horn under gold-colored tape. When Eric sees the hunting horn, he excitedly exclaims, "Wow, a vuvuzela!" I have to laugh, since I know about the African vuvuzela ever since the soccer World Cup in South Africa, where they made every game into a noisy hell. But a German hunting horn and an African vuvuzela seem to be pretty similar, even in shape. Eric and I puff into the horn one after another, the ruckus (yes, we both make a horrid noise) attracting other porters who are also climbing Kilimanjaro with tourists. About fifteen minutes later, a good twenty African porters have tried out the strange instrument and everyone down to the last bird in the forest knows that a German is climbing across Kilimanjaro. There has clearly been a German-African cultural exchange today.

The second day proves to be a bit more difficult. I talk to Eric to feel out how it would look if a tourist suddenly took off to Kenya via the smuggler's route. He explains insistently that there would be serious punishment for anyone who didn't come back down the mountain on the Tanzanian side. I suggest that one could simply neglect to mention a vanished tourist to the national park office. Eric's mood darkens. He brusquely explains that the punishment would be for the tourist as well as the porter, so there is no chance in hell that a porter would return without his tourist. All day I ponder how I could discreetly take off to Kenya without causing any harm to Eric. I don't want it to come back to bite him in any way. But there's no simple solution.

Meanwhile, on day three, we continue to climb relentlessly from 13,000 to 14,000 feet through the clouds toward the snow-capped peak of Kilimanjaro. The air becomes thinner with each foot, until I begin to doubt whether I'm in good enough shape to reach the summit. Every step feels like walking through water, as if there were weights attached to my legs. There is so little oxygen that it feels like I am breathing through a snorkel. I puff and pant while Eric prances up the mountain with the fifty-five-pound parcel, occasionally sounding my hunting horn out of boredom. The fourth day is similar, except Eric has to grab me under the arms repeatedly to keep me from running back down. Without this friendly, motivating service, I probably would have done it.

At the end of the fourth day, we sleep in the last camp at 15,000 feet. We will leave from there to reach the summit of the Kaiser Wilhelm Peak the next morning. Luckily, tourists usually do this last leg without their porter, since it doesn't make much sense to carry fifty-five pounds up to the summit and then immediately back down to the last camp. So I have the perfect chance to make a break for it. But my conscience says, *Don't do it!*

It is with mixed feelings that I say goodbye to Eric at midnight in fourteen-degree cold. I'm dressed in a thick ski suit and a bank robber mask that Eric lends me. He notices my hesitation and asks if I really want to go up to the summit. I nod quickly and disappear into the darkness to climb and stagger for another six hours at angles of thirty to fifty degrees, and from 15,000 to just under 20,000 feet.

Why did I have to start my climb at midnight? I honestly didn't think about it, I just did what everyone does. I just mindlessly followed the other climbers who started the last leg at midnight so that they could see the sunrise from the summit. That sounds romantic, but it really isn't; the six hours to get there are complete hell. You stumble through the rocks with no idea which way is up. And even though I am proud to have achieved it, the thrill people get from this torture remains a mystery to me.

During the torture, I realize that I absolutely can't leave Eric hanging; friendship comes before monetary gain. I know that I am going to return to camp today. But first: to the summit, a childhood dream that I had never imagined would be so difficult.

After hours of cursing myself internally over the crackpot idea of reaching Kenya via Kilimanjaro, the sun finally rises. I'm standing at 5,500 feet, gasping for air like a newborn puppy. But the view from up here is really unbelievable; a sunrise looks a lot better 10,000 feet above the clouds than it does from Costa Brava or somewhere in the middle of Berlin.

The last vertical quarter mile goes by in the warm morning sun. I climb up to the top of Africa by huge glaciers, through scenery that reminds me of the moon. And then I'm standing completely exhausted at 3.5 miles in front of a wooden sign, babbling moronic monologues into my camera.

I'm really happy to have climbed this mountain. I retrieve my German vuvuzela from my backpack to sound a serenade to German-African cultural exchange at the top of the former Kaiser Wilhelm Peak. I only manage a weak toot. Blowing a hunting horn is not really possible at nearly 20,000 feet.

And then I see it: the old smuggling path, between the glaciers. Should I follow it? By now I have no doubt about my answer: *No, I won't do it.*

I wouldn't physically be able to make it down the mountain alone, but more importantly, I can't leave Eric high and dry. What kind of bastard would do that? The next two days are spent heading back down with Eric. I haven't made a trade, but I've made a new friend, which I think is much more important. I finally decide to finance Eric's law studies.

A Pipe in Honor

Back in Arusha, I go through several days of doubt in my venture along with five days of sore leg muscles. I've been walking on a treadmill for weeks: I haven't made one trade and I'm still in Tanzania, which is not good for bartering. A solution occurs to me: the mothership! The state always jumps in when one of its citizens needs help somewhere in the world. Luckily, I'm not in physical, mental, or financial crisis, but I am stuck in a real bartering emergency. I sit at the computer and research the German embassy in Tanzania. I find the honorary consul's email address and relay my concerns in an email. Shortly after, he replies with an invitation to meet. We become friendly quickly, and Ulf empathizes with my bartering crisis; it's obvious that he truly considers himself to be responsible for me.

When I ask where in Tanzania I could put my bartering idea into practice, he first directs me to the past and the German-African exchange in colonial times. Colonialism is never a true exchange; it's certainly not a platform for equal rights, since it always serves the interests of the colonial power. Even if a railroad comes out of it, that part doesn't change.

Then he tells me that the more recent history of the country is marked by many crises. The Tanzanian government traded the entire coffee harvest for oil to keep Tanzania's industry running. According to him, it is a matter of a huge amount of bartered goods that dwarfs any personal exchange. I and my few gold pieces probably couldn't keep up.

A true bartering culture in the private realm really only exists among the countless tribes in the country, as they often live far from big cities and have no real infrastructure as we know it. Additionally, bartering often has an important role in their traditions. That sounds very interesting. Maybe I could pick up my bartering blitz again among the tribes in Tanzania, I think. I ask Ulf what he thinks. As we talk, we are standing in front of an official gold seal with the inscription "Federal Republic of Germany." Ulf leads me through his piece of land, which is official sovereign territory of my country. Then he shows me his coffee plantation, because when Ulf is not busy being the honorary consul, he deals in coffee.

"I could help you," he says suddenly. To my great surprise, he offers me two things: coffee for my labor and a loan of his jeep for a bartering trip to the tribes of Tanzania.

I immediately accept and am beyond happy that my bartering blitz is back on track.

A day later, I stand before a hundred sacks of coffee that each weigh about 130 pounds and each need to be carried by me to the truck standing about eighty feet away. This is my side of the "sack of coffee for labor" trade. My mood is immediately dampened. I've been dealing with acute back pain since the beginning of my trip, and it's finally just begun to go away. But I look over at Ulf, and it's clear that there will be no trade without some sack schlepping.

So I carry one sack after another from storage to the truck, sometimes on my shoulder, sometimes on my back, and occasionally even on my head. But every sack is like a punch in the face, not to mention a punch in my poor back. Other positions such as "pull sack behind me" or "sack on my chest while I scoot backwards across the factory floor" don't help. The weight of the sacks makes my recently-healed back howl in pain again. At sack seventeen I have no choice but to hang up my hat.

Ulf looks at me critically. I can read his thoughts: "Yeah, yeah, a bartering reporter with great ideas and no endurance!"

But he is a polite man. He does nothing to indicate that he doubts my story about back pain. He gives me six sacks of coffee in exchange for the labor and his jeep for a week, even though I haven't touched the remaining eighty-three sacks of coffee—that's what I call diplomatic!

I set off the next day for great adventure in Tanzania with my sacks and my gold and silver coins. It hurts a lot to get in and out of the jeep; my back can't take any more strain, but the trip is gorgeous enough to make up for it. I drive through unbelievable landscapes with high mountains, savannas, and wildlife. At one point, I have to drive at a crawl because of a zebra traffic jam; I don't want to unnecessarily frighten the gentle herd. A day later, on my search for the tribe of the Hadzabe, I end up by the tribe of the Datoga. Many curious faces appear at the window of Ulf's jeep, looking at me with as much surprise as I look at them. The adult men and women wear a lot of elaborate jewelry around their necks, wrists, and ankles. They are dressed in fabric draped around their bodies like cloaks. Their faces are expressive and very attractive with high cheekbones and animated eyes.

In my hand, I have the drawing made for me by an acquaintance, which shows the way to the Hadzabe. It is merely a tree, a hut, and a line that is meant to show the general directions. The Datoga men turn the "map" this way and that in their hands and can make as much of it as I can, which is a shame, yet it comforts me. But the Datoga can help me after all. Alex, one of the tribesmen, vaults into the jeep to show me the way without any bothersome paperwork. That's how I arrive at the Hadzabe tribe.

This tribe is threatened by extinction—it consists of barely one thousand people. Because of the low population, experts say there is much reproduction between not-very-distant relatives. This causes some genetic problems, and that is why they have a tragically high rate of infant death.

The Hadzabe are only about five feet tall and live so traditionally that they still hunt with bows and arrows and live under trees instead of in houses. They wear little clothing and reject modern comforts. They do love to smoke—not tobacco, but let's just say "the Amsterdam stuff."

Onuas, my translator from the village, and I are greeted warmly. I sit in a ring of tribesmen to devote myself to a positive intercultural exchange. But there is a problem: the Hadzabe men sit around smoking together from big pipes, taking one little puff after another. Their big, wooden pipe goes around the circle and is packed with the intoxicant so that no one goes without. After every member of the tribe has smoked excessively, there is a little concert of coughing that doesn't sound entirely healthy. Onuas coughs and wheezes and coughs and wheezes. I am afraid that this little man, who may be fifty-seven, but no one is quite sure, won't be able to breathe anymore. I try to give him a brotherly pat on the back, but that isn't taken so well by the group of coughing, wheezing Hadzabe men. The coughing is part of the ritual for good health.

In the name of cultural exchange, I attempt to take part in this orgy of smoke. After all, in any hippie commune or gang, that's the fastest way to be accepted. But in this moment, I learn that the Hadzabe are very different from such western subcultures: a newbie doesn't get any! As hard as I try to convey my interest, they ignore it. I try to catch the pipe as it makes its rounds. I make some unmistakable gestures (widen my eyes and pretend to smoke a pipe), but the pipe is not shared, the end!

My first evening with the Hadzabe ends with some disappointment and without further exchange. As the sun sets, I sit at the fire under a tree and listen to their poignant chants until I fall asleep.

We get up at six the next morning. I'm generally an early riser, but after a night on the hard ground, I would have liked for the day to begin a bit more gently; that is one of the things that divides life in the wilderness from that of the outside.

While the sun rises, Onuas and the other men sit with me around the fire and show me their bows and arrows, which they use to hunt twice a day. There are three different arrows: the wooden arrow for birds and small animals, the metal arrow for apes, and the poison metal arrow for giraffes and other bigger animals. A poison arrow in the butt means the end. Onuas warns me to be very careful of the poison arrows. He also warns me about the snakes that could be gliding through the brush during the upcoming hunt. Poison arrows and venomous snakes are a bit much for me, so I suggest that I sit out the hunt under the tree with the women and children. Onuas just laughs. It's seems there's never been such an embarrassing situation in the tribe as a man who refuses to take part in the hunt. Onuas assuages my fears about the deadly venomous snake bites. For safety, the men always carry anti-venin with them. (I'm relieved to learn that I might actually wake up after a three-week coma brought on by a snake bite.)

They train me to use the bow and arrow and we shoot at some big objects that even Onuas's eight-year-old grandson can hit—but not me.

Before we leave to hunt, we all sit in a big circle and the splendid pipe makes its way cheerfully around again. Each Hadzabe man inhales powerfully, coughs, wheezes, and passes the pipe to his neighbor. How can this hunt end well when ten intoxicated men are traveling through the snake-infested bush with poison arrows? I feel like I'm in a crazy movie. Nothing makes sense. So when they unexpectedly offer me the pipe this morning, I don't decline. Why not? It can't get any crazier than this, I think. When I inhale through the pipe, I'm overcome with a huge coughing spell. My body and lungs aren't used to so much at once.

As I stand doubled over and coughing in front of a bush, I hear the group of men laughing loudly in the background. They are just as interested in me as I am in them. A short time later we are making our way through the bush in shooting position. I have the metal arrow without poison ready, and I'm mostly occupied with not injuring myself with the poison arrow in my right hand, or poking one of the other men with it. In short, I'm completely stressed out and can only hold myself together by thinking of my end goal: my house in Hawaii!

While crawling (high) through the African bush with a bow and arrow, I realize how far I actually am from my goal. So I ask Onuas in a whisper whether his tribe likes to barter. Onuas, who was just about to shoot a bird, turns toward me, furrows his brow, and asks with a shake of his head whether I would like to go the day without any food. I shut up and try to enjoy the intoxication.

An hour later, we rest by a tree. Onuas and the group break open the bark to find a large amount of honey inside. I'm impressed by how much honey can be hiding in one tree. As we gobble the honey with our sticky hands, Onuas returns to my bartering question. He tells me that the Hadzabe usually trade this honey for arrowheads from their neighboring tribe, the Datoga. The Hadzabe have no way to work with metal.

The second part of the hunt is even more uncomfortable than the first. We have to crawl through thick bush. Not a problem for the five-foot Hadzabe men, but for a six-foot German plagued by back pain, it's a pretty difficult undertaking. I squeeze under the branches, continually losing contact with the group. Before long, I don't know whether the other men are to my left or right or in front of me or behind me. I start to get scared and paranoid that one of their (poison) arrows could suddenly hit me. I call for Onuas. A little later Onuas's eight-year-old grandson comes through the bush to find me. While I was fighting with branches and my back, the little boy had shot a bird and a squirrel, which he shows me proudly.

A little later, we sit around the fire to grill and eat the meager yield. After one bite, my portion is gone. I offer Onuas my matches when the fire goes out but he declines and would rather stick to the traditional method. For the Hadzabe, tradition holds a higher value than technological achievements: life under the trees and with a bow and arrow, freely chosen.

Later, we're standing near the honorary consul Ulf's jeep. I offer to take Onuas out for a joyride. He seems somewhat astonished—he's never been transported by engine power—but he enjoys the drive through the bush and strikes up a song for it. I ask if he would ever accept a car, if not matches. Onuas says that such a car would be great, especially for the women to get to the water hole more quickly, which normally takes from sunrise to sunset. But he declines that help just like the matches. He says that nature is just as important as tradition to the Hadzabe. Everything that is not traditional and is not natural is considered to be relatively uncool. Onuas and I get out of the jeep and he doesn't give it another glance.

As we sit under the tree again for the farewell pipe, I notice a Hadzabe man with a very striking cap. He says that it's a monkey tail cap, made only of the tails of monkeys he killed himself. He also says that a monkey tail cap looks pretty good to Hadzabe women, since it represents manliness. I'm impressed and I think of my bartering. I'm pretty experienced with it at this point, so I offer my cap in exchange for the monkey tail cap. No way! He tells me that the monkey tail caps may not be traded.

I see that I won't get any further with my bartering here. I thank the entire tribe for the wonderful glimpse into their culture. They all sing me a song in farewell, and I'm pulled into a Hadzabe goodbye dance, during which Onuas sings the verses and the rest of the villagers answer with the refrain. All the villagers sing, dance, and clap in a circle. As the mood heats up, the first men jump into the circle to dance. The dance style has a little something of break dancing in it, maybe not as choreographed. I jump into the circle, too, and feel a deep sense of joy at being able to share this unforgettable moment.

Then I drive on to the Maasai, although my heart is still with the Hadzabe. The Maasai tribe is much more internationally famous than the Hadzabe or the Datoga, not least because of books like *The White Masai*. In my research, I found out that the bartering culture of the Maasai is supposed to be much more important than in other tribes, so I stop in one of their villages, which consists of clay huts with tiny slits as window holes. I'm greeted with cheer and music here, too. Mostly by women, who like the Datoga are dressed in flashy jewelry and draped clothing. They tell me that all the men have traveled to a celebration, and so I can arrange any important business directly with them. I explain my bartering journey and my interest in bartering cultures. Two women, Ngonamuna and Naningoi, explain how bartering works among the Maasai.

Both of them were traded by their fathers for four cows when they reached adulthood. I think that I misheard because of the communication hurdles between us, so I politely ask them to repeat themselves. The answer is clear. It's a normal occurrence for the Maasai to trade a woman for a cow. And when a woman can be traded for four cows, she is a particularly good specimen.

I think of *The White Masai*, in which a German woman describes how she fell in love with a Maasai man and moved into his tribe. Quite a few white women later followed this example. I keep hearing here in Africa that suddenly there are western women from America, England, and Germany living in Maasai villages, married to the warriors. I wonder if they knew about the cow trade practice before they moved.

Finally, I get to business and show Ngonamuna and Naningoi my gold, silver, and coffee. They laugh (like Onuas did many times) and tell me that coffee drinking is not really in with the Maasai. So I leave this village, too, without making a trade.

The Fight for Blue Gold

After an unbelievably exciting week in Tanzania, I am still just as far from my next trade as I was when I got here. I have learned a lot about honey and arrowheads and "trade a woman for a cow" culture, but I haven't made another step on my bartering blitz. I sit in my window-less hostel room in Arusha and once again I get that uneasy I'm-in-over-my-head feeling that first developed in India during the tuk-tuk drama. It's an unpleasant feeling that tries to convince me that the whole trip has been a crackpot idea.

After a day of moping, I pull myself together and ask around in my hostel how and where I could possible barter. Pauline, the receptionist, reminds me of tanzanite, which can only be found in Tanzania. I think that's a pretty good idea. Every time that I made a successful trade up, it was for something that was particular to that culture: silk in India, Aboriginal art in Australia, coffee in Tanzania. Because silk has a much higher market value in Australia than in India, I was able to quadruple the value of my item. Pauline gives me three contacts as a starting point for the tanzanite trade: Limo, the taxi driver who allegedly knows everyone; Mr. Buado, the so-called god of the tanzanite business; and a tanzanite trader of the Maasai, who I'll call "Hans Günther" as a precaution, since contacting him turned dangerous for me.

I meet Limo, the taxi driver, who drives me around the block while we chat about the tanzanite scene in Arusha. He warns me about conmen who mostly give tourists fake or poor quality stones. He recommends Punit, an Indian tanzanite dealer who hides behind a big display case full of shining blue stones in his store. We talk, and he thinks a trade for gold, silver, and coffee would be pretty good. Limo and I agree to wait a day to think about the possible risks of the exchange.

So on the next day, I speak to Hans Günther, the tanzanite dealer recommended by Pauline. He immediately and emphatically warns me against Punit, calling him a conman who likes to sell overpriced gems to tourists. I believe him, so distance myself from a trade with Punit.

I still have a third contact to investigate. Mr. Buado, the notorious tanzanite trading god! I meet him in his office, which is armed with bodyguards. A frail man with sunglasses sits behind a desk. He seems somehow unattainable to me, especially after we exchange a few words. I tell him about my interest in bartering and he looks at the gold coins.

"Very nice. I'll take them home to test the quality!" he says.

"No, I don't think so," I answer reflexively, and the short discussion with Mr. Buado is over.

A little later, a young man approaches me on the street corner. Because I'm so desperate, I let myself be taken in. He says that he can help me, and he leads me into a dingy back room in a dingy neighborhood. The dingy back room is the office of the mine owner Mr. Kotago. He sits behind a big desk lamp with a loupe and a pile of precious stones. The atmosphere in this room is like that of a gangster movie. Mr. Kotago has two colleagues next to him, who eye me suspiciously with distrust. The dim light and the few words that are exchanged complete the picture.

Mr. Kotago runs his hand proudly over the big pile of tanzanite on his desk. But unfortunately all the stones are brown and not a glittering blue. When I ask why these stones have this unique color, no one answers. I excuse myself quietly without any further questions.

A little later, I'm with Hans Günther again, drinking coffee. He now offers explicitly to trade for the gold, silver, and coffee. I'm excited, but I keep my guard up. He says that he could give me an eight-carat piece of tanzanite worth $5,000 in Africa and surely double that in western countries. That is exactly what I need, so I ask him to bring me the stone so that I can check its authenticity. Hans Günther is unexpectedly open and trustworthy. He offers to bring me the stone and its certificate of authenticity from a renowned tanzanite institute the next day for me to check out.

The next day, I'm holding an approximately half-inch, glimmering blue stone in my hand. It's somehow so small that you can forget how much it's worth. But I thank Hans Günther for the twenty-four-hour test period. I sit in my hostel room with the stone and a mountain of brochures explaining how to tell the worth of tanzanite: color, cut, shape, weight, and surface quality are important criteria that can quickly bring the value of a stone way up or down. I realize that I'm in over my head. The stone could be worth a million or two old Deutschmarks, and I would never know the difference.

So I go to see Hilde, a German woman who works in tourism in Arusha. I present the stone to her and her ex-husband. I show them the official certificate saying that the stone is eight carats and of the highest quality, AAA. Hilde's raised eyebrows when she sees the certificate lead me to believe I should visit the institute, but under a fake name. If this stone is not actually worth the stated value, there's only one option: Hans Günther must have bribed the examiner.

I enter the institute as "Mike from America." The same examiner whose signature is on Hans Günther's certificate greets me warmly and looks at the stone under his loupe. After examining the weight, form, color, and cut, he shows me the exact market value on a calculator: $2,835. The stone is worth only half as much as Hans Günther and his certificate claim. I ask the examiner why he originally appraised the stone at $5,000 and rated it AAA. He becomes visibly nervous, looks at me in shock, and makes the excuse that $2,835 is the local price and $5,000 is the tourist price. I can tell that he's lying, since he nervously and hastily escorts me to the door. Hans Günther must have bribed him. I can't explain this any other way.

On the one hand, I'm relieved that I haven't officially made the trade yet, but on the other hand, I'm uneasy about what will happen when I confront him about the lie. I'm scared that I've gotten in with a bad crowd, so I decide on a diplomatic solution.

I meet Hans Günther and give him the stone back, explaining that I decided to put off the trade. During the meeting, he is calm and polite. He disappears without many words. But on the following day, I get a text message threatening legal action for wasting his time. In the text, he suggests that I leave the city immediately to avoid any further problems. This threat from a shady gemstone dealer who isn't above bribing an appraiser makes me pretty uneasy. What could happen to me? A lawsuit or maybe just a quick crack on the head, either from him or one of his menacing bodyguards who can always be found walking wordlessly next to him.

I decide to leave the city quickly, but before I leave, I ask a pro for advice in avoiding any more hasty decisions. In a mountain village, I visit the respected Maasai soothsayer Yotasariwaki Samson, who lives in a small clay hut. I ask him to advise me regarding my upcoming bartering. His advice is clear: One: call everyone who you met in Tanzania and offer to trade again! Two: off to Kenya!

I follow his advice and compose a list of all the people I've met in Tanzania:

Ulf, the honorary consul;

Pauline, the receptionist at my hostel;

Eric, the porter from Kilimanjaro (out of the question; his life is already hard enough);

Hilde and her ex-husband;

The tanzanite testing lab (also out of the question, since they're crooked);

The Hadzabe (out of the question due to lack of telephones, same as the Datoga and the Maasai);

Baraka and Limo, taxi drivers;

Mr. Kotago from the back room;

Mr. Buado, the so-called tanzanite god;

Punit, the Indian;

Hans Günther (out of the question since he threatened to sue).

Then I call all those who haven't been ruled out, even though it feels uncomfortable. Their answers are all similar: "Hmmm . . . well . . . Uh, no, I'm so busy . . . The water's boiling, got to go . . . Hello? I can't hear you."

It goes on like that until I have Hilde on the phone. Completely unexpectedly, she invites me, my three ounces of gold, the three ounces of silver, and the sacks of coffee to her office.

A Ten-Thousand-Dollar Piece of Paper

Hilde, a woman in her fifties, left Germany twenty-five years ago to follow her childhood dream: to roar through the Serengeti regularly in her own Jeep. And she's regularly done just that and also opened a travel agency in Tanzania. Here she sits in her travel office, which could be described as retro. Aside from the old furniture, a typewriter from the seventies, and an equally old telephone, I'm struck by the colors: brown and bright orange. Hilde herself, on the other hand, is not at all retro. She is a woman who always looks younger than she really is. She dresses young, seems to have a fresh sense of humor, and seems uncomplicated when it comes to the topic of bartering.

She tells me that she likes to barter. In return for her nanny's labor, she had a house built for her. I'm impressed by this truly generous example of bartering and realize I have a big chance here after all my bad luck. I show her one of the 130-pound coffee sacks to represent all of them, and place the three gold and three silver thalers in her hand.

Hilde looks at them with interest, sitting behind her desk. She starts to spin the coins on the glass desk, and I hear them clinking against it over and over. I gasp a little each time, since a crack in the coin could cause a serious loss of value. I politely suggest that maybe playing tops is not so good, but Hilde grins and explains that she would like to keep the coins. I'm relieved and immediately discuss the exchange.

She offers me a travel voucher for two for a three-week adventure trip through Tanzania on Hilde's dime. After about three minutes of negotiation, we've put together a travel packet that allows the trader to relive my own Tanzanian journey. I summarize it all in the form of a collage on a big card.

Voucher for Travel in Wigge's Footsteps at a Value of $10,000

For Two People:

Flight to Tanzania
6 day Kilimanjaro climb with my hunting horn and lederhosen—
Eric will also be in your party
A wildlife safari day
Visit to the Hadzabe, Maasai, and Datoga; includes hunt
Overnight in my (windowless) hostel room
Mountain climb training complete with sweatband and mango lifts
at the market in Arusha
Visit to the Maasai soothsayer
Coffee sack carrying for coffee manufacturer
Meeting with tanzanite dealer including bamboozling
Trip lasts just under three weeks

I'm extremely excited about this development. With this trade, I've doubled the value of my gold, silver, and coffee, when just a few days ago I almost halved it with Hans Günther and the rigged jewel.

Additionally, I'm quite sure that I can easily trade this voucher on a brief stopover in Germany. With an intermediate result of $10,000 at the halfway point of my trip, I have good prospects for making it to a house in Hawaii by the end. My apple was worth seventy-nine euro cents, so about a dollar, which I've now multiplied by ten thousand.

After briefly throwing my arms around Hilde in gratitude, I immediately pack my things to get out of Arusha quickly. I don't want to fall into the heavily armed (in my imagination at least) hands of Hans Günther so that he can obligingly take my $10,000 coupon.

I can finally leave Tanzania for Kenya with a clear conscience, just like the Maasai soothsayer said. I don't count on there being any chance of my making this trade there, but since I'm in such good standing, I can devote a few days of my mission to learning more about cultural exchange and bartering.

10

A WORLD-CLASS RUNNER
AMONG PEERS

Kenya

I drive through Nairobi to the mountain town of Eldoret, which has enjoyed some fame due to generating so many Kenyan highland runners. Almost all Kenyan runners who earned gold medals in the 800, 3,000, 5,000, and 10,000 meters as well as the marathon distance come from here. Eldoret is almost 6,000 feet high in the mountains and most of the residents are members of the Nandi tribe. The mixture of altitude and residents who are gifted athletically and in endurance creates a class of athletes that is one of a kind. They make other nations look pretty old and slow.

I contact Frank, a TV satellite installer who knows every gold-medal winner in town—the runners obviously belong to the financial upper class and can afford to have satellite TV. Frank helps me meet three of the best athletes so that I can talk to them about what they've learned about intercultural exchange from their careers and whether—purely hypothetically—they would ever barter their gold medals.

I first meet Joseph Keter, who won gold in the 300-meter hurdle in the 1996 Olympic Games in Atlanta. He's in his early forties, humorous, and lives in a surprisingly modest house. It stands among a landscape that I had never expected in Kenya. Because of the altitude, the region is very rainy, fertile, and temperate, almost like Germany. There are forests, fields, and cows, just like in the Black Forest or Sauerland, except this place is strangely right on the equator, and of course I haven't seen a cuckoo clock anywhere.

Joseph seems to have remained a totally normal and likeable guy despite his gold medal. He's easy to kid around with, but my mission requires me to get serious again. He tells me that his sports career brought him to over fifty countries. He came into contact with so many different cultures and technological developments that they still don't have in Kenya. Cultural exchange did a lot for him personally, and he can pass on his knowledge to the surrounding villages, for example, to help make progress in agriculture.

I see a pretty wooden box in his living room. The gold medal must be in there, I think. Joseph picks up the box and grins at me. It's empty. No medal. He explains that he keeps it in the bank so that nobody gets any ideas about stealing it. He shakes his head emphatically when I ask if he would trade his gold medal for anything. He wants it to inspire his children to reach their goals as well.

He suggests that I visit a good friend of his who lives right around the corner. Paul Bitok is also a gold medal winner in African championships and a two-time silver medal winner at the 1992 and 1996 Olympics in the 5,000-meter race.

We drive over sludgy dirt roads to a very poor village with noticeably large buildings on its outskirts. They are Paul's apartment buildings; like many other runners, he put his money into real estate. It's strange to see five-floor office buildings stuck among the poor houses and huts.

Paul reminds me that in the 5,000-meter race in 1993, he was beaten in the home stretch by a German. That's right; Dieter Baumann surprisingly won the gold. I can still remember the scene very well, watching the finals live on my TV as a fifteen-year-old, just like so many other Germans. One hundred and fifty meters before the finish line, Dieter Baumann was in fourth place behind the African runners. It was clear that our man had no chance against Kenya's star lineup, especially since the Africans' best times were significantly better than his. But Baumann was known for his strong sprint, so he managed to dash forward through a small gap in the last fifty meters, passing Paul. The excitement in Germany was huge, since the Kenyans were considered practically invincible.

As Paul tells the story with a photo of the home stretch in his hand, the mood becomes sentimental and a bit sad. After all, Paul had to trade his gold medal for a silver one in the last moment, even though the gold was almost close enough to touch. I ask if that left him with any frustration, but Paul sees everything in a very positive and friendly light. He says that second place is much better than any place after that. I'm impressed that unlike so many others, he can be happy about something other than a gold medal. Many athletes and even fans see second place as defeat. Only winners are celebrated, at least that's how it seems to me in our society. I ask Paul why he and his colleagues left room for Baumann in the final stretch; they could have easily closed the space. Paul says that the fastest one should win, so there was no reason to do that. These statements truly move me, so I feel sort of sleazy when I ask about the hypothetical medal trade. Paul says that he wouldn't trade his medal for a million dollars; its sentimental value is immeasurable.

I have him sign my self-made $10,000 travel voucher to raise its value a little. Then I drive back to Eldoret with Frank the satellite installer to meet the master of all masters, the champ, the guru of track, simply the best of the best: Moses Kiptanui, seven-time gold medalist and seven-time world record holder. I can still remember his career clearly. In the nineties, he dominated the running world in long distances.

I meet Moses in a huge office building in the center of poor-looking Eldoret. All the residents of the town know to thank the hero for this investment. I'm received on the fifth floor by his manager, who leads me into his office, where a friendly, grinning man in a suit is sitting. It's Moses, the man I saw make so many world-class runners look feeble in so many championships when I was a teenager. I get right to the barter question:

"Moses, would you trade your gold medal for something great?"

"Absolutely not!"

"What if someone with a $10,000 travel voucher came by?"

"Definitely not for that!"

"You can think about your answer a little."

"Listen, gold medals can't be traded. They are a symbol of the outstanding achievements that I accomplished, and they should be an example to the other people in the town."

Moses signs the voucher, but naturally we don't make a trade. What would anyone in Kenya want with a Tanzanian travel voucher? That would be sort of like trading for a trip to North Dakota when you live in South Dakota.

Good, good, I understand: medals are not to be traded, but to serve as motivation for others!

After these touching encounters with real gold medalists, I drive back to my hostel to pack my things. I have to bring my travel voucher to Germany. On the way to the hostel, my cell phone rings. It's Joseph Keter, who has done some soul-searching and has a good sense of humor. He would like to undo the shame of the 1992 Olympic finals against Dieter Baumann. He says that this is the chance for him to finally get a hold of a German in Kenya. He wants revenge for Kenya, and I will have to fight him for it. Surprised and bewildered, I ask what Joseph means. "You against me, eight hundred meters, just us. Or don't you think you can do it?"

Me against a former Olympic gold medalist? Unbelievable! Of course I will represent Germany with dignity, there's no question. Who would turn down an opportunity for such a world-class race?

We meet in the venerable Eldoret stadium where so many talents, medal winners, and world record setters began their careers. The stadium is a bit understated. There is only a cinder track, a small wooden scaffold for bleachers, a cow on the soccer field, and a farmer who for unknown reasons continually starts and stops his tractor, disturbing the runners. This afternoon there is also a group of prisoners from the Eldoret jail pulling weeds from the track. They are wearing classic black-and-white-striped prison clothing like I've only seen in movies, but they are not chained. Their warden tells me that he trusts them all, even though some are serious offenders.

Between cows, broken bleachers, the farmer and his tractor, and the prisoners without chains, I see all sorts of famous people, like the 800-meter world record holder Rudisha, who is training briskly by himself. I talk to a few different runners who all have mid- and long-distance times that many professional German athletes could only dream of.

Then I see Joseph walking slowly into the stadium as if in slow motion. The slow-mo effect is interrupted by other people who speak to him excitedly, since he is a great man in Eldoret and an example for many.

Joseph shakes my hand and asks me with a wink if I'm prepared. I tell him that I just climbed Kilimanjaro as training, but I could hardly begin to match his performance. Joseph grins. I ask him if we can make the race a little bit fairer. Joseph is reasonable, so he agrees to carry my travel pack, filled with sixteen one-liter water bottles, which is about thirty-seven pounds. I find it only fair that we should start at the same weight, I with 176 pounds of body weight, and he with 139 pounds of body weight plus 37 in the backpack.

Now we begin trying to intimidate each other for half an hour. Joseph warms up, does professional stretches, weird jumps, and other things that one normally does before an Olympic final. I can't think of anything better to do than walk up and down the sprint track and do some so-called jack-knife sit-ups in between. I saw the exercise once on a morning television program and heard a woman with a sweatband say that you could look twenty at the age of fifty if you do it regularly. My jack knife exercise seems to impress Joseph very little. He wants to get started and undo the shame caused by Dieter Baumann. We stand at the starting line, ready to run twice around the 400-meter track. One of the three observers gives us the signal to start, and off we go. The commentary during live coverage of this grandiose race would have gone something like this:

On your marks, get set, go!

Wigge shoots forward at an amazing speed, grinning in certainty of his win. Keter has difficulties and struggles with his sixteen water bottles. Keter is now an unbelievable thirty meters behind. Wigge runs and runs. The distance between the runners grows: fifty meters, sixty meters. Keter is way behind, now running with one hand on the backpack. What a grandiose defense of Germany's title in the name of Dieter Baumann. Outsider Wigge must have trained in secret.

But now Wigge is distracted by the tractor—What is that tractor doing here?—and loses his rhythm. Keter immediately uses his chance, the fans cheer, even the prisoners are amazed, Keter begins to catch up, and Wigge gets nervous. He's in over his head. Keter now running completely without arm movement, what a strange running style. Still twenty meters behind. Wigge looks around, Keter closes in, he sees a gap—just like Dieter Baumann. Close it up, Wigge, close it up! But no, Keter pulls past and beats Wigge. Wigge falls onto the finish line and Germany is beaten. Kenya has restored her honor. Germany is beaten . . .

I lay completely beaten, wheezing, sweating, and panting behind the finish line. Joseph walks over to me, relaxed and grinning, stretches out his hand to me in a gesture of German-Kenyan reconciliation, and gives me a friendly hug.

It's a great moment that makes us both happy. Me, because I never expected that I'd lose to a real Olympic gold medalist by just a few tenths of a second, and Joseph, of course because now he can finally leave the scandal of 1992 behind him. What better thing could I contribute to international trade?

11

HOME SWEET HOME

Germany

Now I sit on a flight from Nairobi to Frankfurt with my travel voucher and a serious muscle ache. I'm in a good mood since I am expecting some good trade opportunities on my stopover in Germany. I have a variety of strategies for making people aware of this great chance for a travel voucher barter.

The Internet: I'll produce a video and publish it on my travel blog to win over my readers with an attractive moving image. I'll post the same video on Facebook (I have 651 "friends" by this point). Additionally, I'll post ads in over twenty travel and bartering forums.

The Street: After four months on my bartering blitz, this is my area of expertise: talking to people, keeping them interested, and convincing them to barter. I'm fully confident that I am up for the challenge.

The Media: I've been working in media for ten years and have a few contacts. So I send inquiries to twenty newspapers, radio stations, and TV programs proposing an interview.

"What could possibly go wrong with such a wide-ranging master plan?" I ask myself.

In the Berlin summer, almost two weeks go by with the same rhythm: computer on, check blog for comments, check the travel forums, send emails to the media, check Facebook, and turn the computer off in frustration. And then I do something that I never wanted to do. To improve my disappointing days without any offers of barter, I start smoking again! An unbelievable faux pas. A relapse at the age of thirty-four! But this disappointment over my failing trade offers caught me off guard. Empty beer bottles and piles of cigarette butts start to gather on my desk—the picture of a totally frustrated reporter.

Since no offers seem to want to appear through electronic means, I move on to my second strategy, the street. I stand at the Brandenburg Gate, in the Sony Center, in front of the Reichstag, in Potsdamer Platz, and wherever else with the five-by-three-foot voucher in my hand. I shout the same thing over and over to the crowd:

"Voucher for travel to Africa for two people! Three weeks! Kilimanjaro climb included! Yes, you heard right! Kilimanjaro! Kilimanjaro! Kilimanjaro!"

As I stand there in the crowd, I notice a catty, grumpy voice taking over in my head:

"Yeah, take this stupid Kilimanjaro trip. This damn, difficult trip. The trip where I spent six days climbing this mountain even though I hate hiking. This trip where a line of jewel dealers tried to fleece me. Oh yeah, and take the trip where I was laughed at by the Hadzabe just because I didn't know how to smoke their big weed pipe. Just take it . . ."

It feels like there's something screaming in my head, "Take this trip, then I'll finally be rid of it!" And then I think: that's not what I want. When did I get so bitter about all the amazing experiences in the recent past? One thing is clear: in this mood, I'll never get anyone to take this trip. If I'm projecting what I'm thinking right now, no fish will bite.

I also notice that I'm completely exhausted and need a break so that I can remember everything in a good light again and communicate that to potential trade partners. I can't do it like this, that much is clear, so I end my street peddling.

Since the Internet is still only bringing me uninteresting or dubious trade offers, I reach out to my media contacts. I write to as many editors and presenters as possible and ask for an exciting interview about the last four months' bartering blitz, during which I can make a call for trades.

I hear my colleagues say "We should meet for coffee," and I hear myself ask "What's going on?" or "What have you been up to?" And just like on the street, I feel nothing but exhaustion and a strange emptiness. I notice that I'm not being earnest. I like all the people I'm speaking to, but honestly, with time running short, I have no desire for a friendly chat and no energy to listen to other people's stories. And naturally, other people notice that. I don't have to wait long for the results. Two days later, I find two rejections in the mailbox, and silence from others. The bartering blitz doesn't seem to interest anyone, not in the middle of the summer slump.

I slowly begin to get nervous. I have just a few days in Germany and then I have to get on my next flight, this time to Ukraine. I check all the online platforms again and keep chain-smoking. Then I get the first interesting offers through my blog. There is a reader who wants to trade her Mercedes 230 from the nineties and an older lady who wants to trade her old coins from the South Pacific for the Africa trip. But I have to pass on both offers.

The Mercedes is too difficult logistically. What happens if I can't get rid of it in Ukraine? South America is still on the itinerary. Should I drive across the Atlantic in a Mercedes? That's way too difficult with all the import regulations in the various countries. I have to pass on the South Pacific coins because although the sentimental value for their owner may be high—they come from a honeymoon long past—they don't have enough value for me.

At three in the afternoon, just as I am about to open my second pack of cigarettes for the day, an offer for an interview comes from a radio show. I'm relieved that someone finds my story at least halfway interesting. On Friday evening I sit in the studio with a funny young host, talking about my crocodile tests in Australia, tuk-tuk craziness in India, and the almost successful trip into Kenya via Kilimanjaro. The host is very excited and makes room in the program for me to put out a call to barter. I advertise, I plead, I demand, I convince, I enthrall, I do everything in my forty-five seconds to get my travel voucher out to the people.

A day later my mailbox still yawns open, empty. Is Germany just not a bartering country? Or is my trip to Africa just not attractive enough for someone to lay seven thousand euros on the table?

At any rate, I notice that the euphoria I originally had for the travel voucher was clearly unjustified. I'll never get rid of the thing.

Two days before my flight, I again browse half-heartedly through all the travel forums on which I posted my bartering notices. And then this:

"I would like to trade with you. Best wishes, Diana!"

My cigarette falls onto the keyboard from pure shock and surprise, leaving me with a lasting bartering blitz memory.

A little later I call up Diana and she tells me that she is an artist who would like to trade her paintings. I am skeptical of art as a bartering item, since the value is always subjective, but I still hop in my car and drive to Salzgitter in Lower Saxony.

Diana shows me her paintings in her grandma's basement. They are all on three-by-four-foot canvases, and are very attractive to my layman's eyes. During the negotiations, Diana tells me that she gave up her career as an artist for a job as an art therapist and that she is not internationally known.

I feel worries flooding my soul. What if I can't get rid of the paintings? What if I come home after the last eighty-five days of my trip with *nothing*? What if the nouveau riche in Ukraine laugh at me? I look inside myself and then I say no to Diana, even though I'm sorry about it.

Diana is more than a little impressed by that. She shows me a certificate for an art prize and flyers from various exhibitions. Unfortunately, I have to remain firm.

But then I suddenly get an idea. "Let's just trade your art for mine!" I offer, looking at her with an expectant, wolfish grin.

Diana finally agrees to me painting her a forty-by-twenty-inch painting in exchange for two of hers, right here and now in her grandma's basement. I decide to portray the crocodile-feeding scene in Australia and get painting. I very soon notice Diana furrowing her brow. She was expecting a talented painter. Yes, I admit that my painting has not developed much since the end of my grade school days. I immortalize the crocodile, sun, man, and the sparse greenery in this style.

Diana keeps her composure, even says thank you, and completes the trade. Two excellent paintings are added to the travel voucher.

I finally carry my items through the entrance hall of the Berlin airport, where I take another important step. I stop smoking again. The great bartering crisis is at an end. Thanks, Diana!

12

ILLUSORY BEAUTY

Ukraine

My heavy bags and I land in Odessa on the Black Sea coast in high summer. The city impresses me: sun, beach, beautiful architecture from bygone epochs, and beautiful women everywhere. I can hardly believe how much beauty goes by me in just a few seconds. Long legs, short skirts, tall women, some blonde, some brunette, some pretty, and some even prettier. I feel paralyzed. I can't keep my mind on bartering. Could this be my reward for all the difficulties of my trip? Are all these beautiful women here just for me?

A young woman in a café pulls me out of my fantasies and back to reality when she explains that there are so many beautiful women here and that the city is known for it far and wide because the sex business is booming. Many women are not from Odessa, but followed their job in the erotic trade here. Once I know that, I'm almost a bit ashamed at so blindly succumbing to feminine charms. It's just that I'm not used to having so much beauty around me. Even though I don't like to admit it, I have a hard time getting back to business.

Since trying to barter on the street is a total failure due to lack of a common language (people only speak Russian), I look for trade partners online and in the process, I stumble on disturbing facts that have to do with unsafe interpersonal exchange in Odessa. Allegedly, the HIV infection rate is the highest in all of Europe. I gulp. I continue to research. Why have so many people here been infected? And what does that mean for sexual exchange between people in Odessa?

I meet with Alexander at the local Caritas, who brings me to an HIV clinic. The doctor tells me that approximately 7.5 percent of the population is HIV positive, including unreported cases. That means that about 75,000 people are infected. I can hardly believe it. There are about 70,000 HIV positive people in all of Germany. More HIV patients in one city than in all of Germany with its more than eighty million people! How could I have naively believed in a city of dream women?

Alexander brings me to Katja, who contracted HIV seven years ago. She tells me that the sex industry in Odessa definitely plays a big part in it, and that many tourists only come for that reason. Then she tells me about her own situation. Community relationships are often very limited, since HIV is still taboo despite the circumstances. She says that even doctors have shunned her, and that it was difficult to find a kindergarten for her children.

Later I meet Olga, who contracted HIV eleven years ago and has a seven-year-old HIV negative daughter. I didn't know that was possible. She explains that medication had kept the virus count in her blood so low that her daughter, Lina, could come into the world without the disease. Her next candid statement blows me away even more: even though she regularly has unprotected sex with her husband, he is still negative. That's because of the same reason: the pills keep the virus in check. It's still pretty incomprehensible to me that they don't use condoms.

I take a walk around the city in the evening sun and I can hardly enjoy the beauty or the beauties. As I see the masses of people strolling cheerfully through the city, I wonder if they are all really as happy as it appears at first glance.

Exchange of Religions

As I walk around the city a little later, I notice something else: the city seems to be a multicultural meeting point; people from over a hundred different nations live here. This cultural diversity can be seen in the various houses of worship: synagogues, mosques, and churches are everywhere. I decide to research this topic a little more, so that I can understand how exchange between religions works. In Odessa, these religions have been coexisting peacefully for centuries, which can't be said about every place in the world. I've often thought that everything would be much easier if there was just one single world religion. Is that true? And of course, I hope my foray into religion will allow me to make a few exciting trades.

First stop: an Orthodox Christian convent. To promote religious exchange, I take part in the service and learn that here they drink the holy water instead of dabbing themselves with it. The Orthodox nun Katherina tells me that she thinks that differences in faith are important, because the diversity creates conversations about God.

In farewell, she gives me two orthodox convent books.

I can't do too much with that statement, so I visit the Lutheran church, where I am surprisingly greeted by the German pastor Herr Hamburg. As I explain my trading project, he sets me up as a sexton: sexton's cowl, carrying the Bible to the altar, and laying the host on a plate—those are just a few of the things that are supposed to bring me closer to his religion.

I ask Herr Hamburg if it wouldn't be better if all religions were melded into one. Pastor Hamburg counters that he likes my green t-shirt, but also likes his white shirt. He also agrees that the diversity of religion provides an opening for exchange. At the same time, he admits that everything good has its downside, and that there unfortunately are black sheep among the religious, who make exchange difficult.

And because he loves the colorful things in life, he likes my two paintings, especially the most colorful one. He wants to trade right away. I'm surprised that I don't have to spend a lot of time convincing him, but rather can get right to the point.

Pastor Hamburg comes out of the sacristy with two Bibles, one from the nineteenth century and one from the eighteenth, so probably three hundred years old. I can choose one of the two. I really like the older bible, even though it is a little tattered, so I choose that one. On the same day, I buy a wooden box to raise the value a little with serious packaging and to avoid any further damage.

I head to the city's synagogue with the travel voucher, the one painting, the three-hundred-year-old Bible, and the two convent books. I take part in the service here, too, but I quickly realize that my plan has backfired. All around me, believers stand and sit, pray from the Torah, and bow. I don't understand anything and I feel uneasy about simply going along without first being taught about the rituals and customs. Interestingly, my fidgeting doesn't disturb anyone. The atmosphere is relaxed and seems to leave enough room for people who just want to watch, despite all the rituals.

After the service, Rabbi Wolf laughs at how embarrassed I am, and gives me a fatherly pat on the shoulder. In our conversation, I ask him whether the huge number of religions really encourages exchange or just stirs up conflict. After all, it can't be denied that religion has played a huge role in so many world conflicts. Rabbi Wolf explains that faith supports solidarity between people in the community and brings together all classes and professions. He unfortunately doesn't go into the fact that there are also religious wars.

As a sign of inter-religious exchange, he gives me a Torah with the five books of Moses, and takes my Orthodox convent book.

I continue on, this time to a mosque, with my Torah, the three-hundred-year-old Bible, the travel voucher to Africa, and the big painting. I don't want to go through the same disgrace as I did in the Jewish congregation, so I ask for a little orientation. I am introduced to the prayer along with the children of the mosque. After washing our hands and feet, twenty children and I sit in the prayer room and practice Muslim prayer. As a gesture of exchange, the Imam gives me a Muslim head covering. He looks happy to see how quickly I've integrated myself into his mosque.

When we talk, I ask him, too, if a single world religion wouldn't solve a lot of problems and might support exchange between people. Surprisingly, he agrees, and tells me that we are already on the way to one religion. The big world religions of Judaism, Christianity, and Islam are closely related to each other. The Old Testament is the basis for Christianity as well as Judaism. Jesus is the son of God for Christians and a prophet for Muslims. The three religions are much more similar than one might think. The goal of unity and easy exchange is visible. I'm really impressed; I had not expected this statement of support for exchange.

My most recent encounters have brought me much understanding of the sense of faith and religious diversity, even though I personally have not become a believer. But now it's time to turn back to the theme of bartering again.

Wife-swap

I prepare my arguments for trading the painting:

Painting as tabletop: someone has to go under the painting to serve as a support. I tried it in the pedestrian area of Odessa, and it worked. A young woman immediately felt compelled to set her drink on the human table.

Painting as fan: can be used to cool down in the summer heat. This option was also tested successfully with pedestrians.

Painting as a shield against the attack of the Pleiadians: maybe it's not very likely for someone to end up in this situation, but after my visit to the UFO fans in Switzerland, I know anything is possible.

Painting as camouflage: if you hide behind it, you're invisible. Detectives will love it.

Painting as reflector: wrapped in reflective foil, ideal for sunbathing.

But my walk around the city becomes disappointing, because despite the diversity of nationalities, only a few people speak English and no one wants to barter with me. I disappointedly plan my further travels to the Ukrainian capital city of Kiev, where allegedly there are many newly rich millionaires. After the fall of communism in the early nineties, they earned a ton of money in oil or in other businesses that we don't talk about.

Just before I'm about to set off, I get a very surprising email from a Peter in Portugal, who only just saw my call for trades in Germany. I call him, and we become friendly very quickly even though he is over seventy. He tells me that he is financially set and doesn't need anything on his estate in Portugal, but would love to trade something. I tell him that I would happily free him of some of his property, and we ponder what he could get from me.

"The Bible?"

"No, thanks. I already have two eighteenth-century Bibles."

"The painting?"

"No, thanks, I can't fit any more art in my house!"

"The travel voucher?"

"Oh, I've traveled so much, you know. Please not that."

Peter is so wealthy that none of my things excite him. I try to keep him on the phone with offers of service, thinking back to the tests of courage in Australia and the coffee sack schlepping in Africa, but Peter turns me down and says goodbye. Before he hangs up, he makes a little joke: "Michael, just come stop by in Portugal, maybe you'll have a beautiful Ukrainian woman in your bag!"

I think about that. No, an Eastern European woman is not something I can trade; I'm not in the business of human trafficking. But a little bit later I get a glorious idea! Even if I can't bring a pretty Ukrainian girl to Portugal, I can still summon them to Peter's living room. That may sound contradictory, but it isn't.

Two days later, I sit on a sofa in the office of a German-Ukrainian marriage service in the city of Vinnitsa. The agency boss Tanja explains a few things about the popular intercultural marriages. It is apparently always Ukrainian women and western men who want to meet. Ukrainian men and western women don't work out. Intercultural exchange is only a side note, though; it's much more about the trade of beauty for security.

Life and Death Trade

It's no wonder, considering the disastrous economic situation: an English teacher earns a hundred euros a month, even though the cost of living in Ukraine is not much lower than in Germany. Emigrating to the EU without a marriage is almost impossible. If you don't have children, a lot of money, or a good job, the gates of the EU remain closed. It's not easy.

I saw this dilemma with my own eyes a few days prior in the prohibited zone of Chernobyl. I booked a tour in the radiated region to get an idea of whether any form of exchange is still possible there after the reactor accident in 1986. My tour guide was twenty-two-year-old Vita, who told me about herself. I quickly forgot the abandoned, radiated buildings and was much more interested in why Vita worked here and lived half the month in the radiation contaminated town of Chernobyl. The answer is simple: she went to college, speaks fantastic English, and has plenty of other qualifications, but none of the available jobs pay more than a hundred euros a month. That's why she lives in this radiation hell two weeks out of the month, guiding journalists through the Red Forest, a forest which is still radioactive with up to forty microsieverts. You aren't allowed to stay there more than a few minutes. But Vita does it, gets paid six hundred euros a month, and had to sign a three-year contract.

What kind of consequences will this have for her? Will she be able to have children? I left the prohibited zone with a sadness that I have seldom experienced on this trip—I met a young, attractive, highly qualified woman who is trading her health for six hundred euros a month because the economic situation in her country is so terrible.

After this experience, I tell Tanja, the marriage broker, about Peter's joke trade suggestion, but I also consider that it is probably inappropriate, considering the serious situation in Ukraine. Tanja has a great idea: she knows two women who are a little better off financially and would like to play along with the bartering blitz. These two young Ukrainian women will soon be seen in Peter's living room in Portugal. . . .

The same day, Ina, Marina, and I stand in front of Vinnitsa's attractions, consisting of a water tower, a park, and a town square. Ina and Marina are both in their mid-twenties, attractive, and speak German. We begin with a very personal video production for Peter with Ina and

Marina in the starring roles. "Hello Peter, this is Ina and Marina with a veeery personal city tour just for you!"

In a short film, they show the unknown man in Portugal the water tower, which Peter should visit, then they show him the "Central Park" of Vinnitsa, and the a square called Parisian Square.

Ina and Marina are not shy about talking to Peter in their very personal and tender way, as if they were two of his admirers. Musical interludes, kisses in slow motion, and some erotic posing at the water tower, which they call Big Ben, round it all out. I cut it together with my cameramen Dominik and Jakob, amp up the atmosphere with slow motion and animated hearts, and hope that it knocks Peter out of his seat when I offer him this video in trade.

Thirty-six Hours

With my travel voucher, painting, Bible, the five books of Moses, and the vaguely erotic DVD in a little treasure chest, I travel on to Kiev. I want to use my last thirty-six hours in Ukraine to make a final trade in this country.

As I leave the apartment that I've rented, I hardly believe my eyes. The nouveau riche are everywhere! In the street, Porsches are parked behind BMWs, and Mercedes behind Rolls Royces. It is a sight that I have rarely seen. Dolled up women with little dogs and Louis Vuitton bags shove past each other on the street. I set down my travel pack quickly. Now is my chance to trade Diana's painting. As much as I like it, it's too big and bulky for my trip.

I soon begin canvassing the rich and beautiful, but I always get the same reaction: silence! Apparently bartering is seen as uncool among the upper class. I finally get the important tip that I should give working a try. When I am about to move on, I get an extra tip, that I should try the Andreevsky bridge, since art is sold there.

I go there and I see piles of paintings hanging on the walls, but no potential buyers near or far. This bridge, which is just called a bridge but is actually a street, has a huge supply and no demand. I see a few art sellers who frown angrily, taking me to be new competition. I know that I won't get any further here, and I'm about to give up when a young woman interested in my painting suddenly speaks to me. I ask what she has to barter. She gestures toward her bag. I wait and watch her hand slide into it. What will it be? A bottle of expensive champagne, a pound of caviar, or maybe the long-desired Rolex worth 10,000 euros? She slowly pulls her hand back out of the big purse. I see the first glimpse of the item. It is white and looks like the neck of a bottle, like a yogurt bottle—to be specific, it is a white plastic bottle filled with kefir. The young woman starts laughing. I walk away silently and am really annoyed. I only have one more day before I leave Ukraine, and jokes like that don't seem funny to me.

In the apartment, I click through the Internet in frustration, search "millionaire Kiev" and "rich and bored in Kiev," and continue my search for the wealthy that I began in Berlin. At first I just read nonsense, but then I discover the Ukrainian pop icon Ruslana in my documents. I had called her manager weeks before regarding my bartering trip. Now it's time to get serious.

Secret Trade

A few people will surely still remember Ruslana. She won the 2004 Eurovision Song Contest and enjoyed some hype across Europe. Ruslana also won the World Music Award and got involved politically with the Orange Revolution in Ukraine. She has become a sort of folk hero. On her website, I find the contact info for her manager, who I call up explaining that the bartering blitz could be huge for Ruslana. I argue that intercultural exchange is a must for an internationally known pop star. The manager says no because Ruslana is invited to visit the president of Kazakhstan the next day, so she can't barter. But I keep the manager on the phone with more arguments for German-Ukrainian understanding, and explain how important this meeting could be. The manager tries to get out of it because Ruslana is currently rehearsing to be a jury member for a TV show that could be called "Ukrainian Idol." I grab the smallest opportunity in her refusal: "No problem, I'll just come over there and wait until she has a little break!"

The manager hesitates, but doesn't want to anger a foreign journalist, so she agrees. Two and a half hours go by backstage on "Ukrainian Idol" until Ruslana sees me. I know that for any Eastern European, meeting her would be like meeting God, so I must be exceedingly polite. We talk about my bartering trip and my desire to trade with a famous personality such as her. Ruslana seems excited, but also signals that she doesn't really need to have the painting. I start to panic that this amazing trade opportunity with a pop star could crumble so quickly. A spontaneous emergency lie comes out of me: "Actually, there is a wolf in the painting painted especially for you by a German artist, because you wore wolf pelts at the Eurovision Song Contest and also sang about wolves."

Ruslana is flattered and happy that a painting was painted especially for her. I know that it's not good to lie, but under the pressure of the bartering blitz, I let myself get carried away. (Sorry, Ruslana!)

Ruslana gets her tambourine out of her bag, which she had with her at Eurovision, and starts to sing. I try making some music with the tambourine, but it sounds pretty ridiculous, so she discreetly takes the instrument away from me. She wants to trade the tambourine for the "wolf painting."

I politely explain that the tambourine is awesome, but I need items that have physical and not just sentimental value, since I am on the way to a house in Hawaii. I also know that I have to offer something else.

"If you can trade something more valuable, I'll fly out tomorrow with you to Kazakhstan and work as your luggage carrier!"

Ruslana is astonished by my offer and wants to accept right away, but her manager, who naturally is accompanying her, steps in: "No, we are definitely not taking him with us. No way!" I try to convince her, make jokes, plead, explain what a great benefit I would be to her on the trip, and implore her: "Please, I really need to trade up!"

There is a short silence in the room and it's now clear to everyone how important a good trade is for me. Ruslana breaks the awkward silence, offering to meet me the next day by the Vudybichi train station under the three highway overpasses, which she will be passing on her way to the airport. She will bring her barter item with her, but it will be a secret. I agree and am happy to have come so far.

The next morning at eleven, I stand by the Vudybichi subway station under the three highway overpasses on the edge of Kiev. The area is surreal, with highways, bridges, garbage, trucks, and a few shadowy figures on the side of the road. I feel like I'm in a bad gangster movie making a secret trade of "weapons for drugs" or "weapons for drugs and a body."

But there is one big difference between this and a film. There, everyone, whether gangsters or undercover cops, shows up more or less on time, but not here. I wait over an hour for Ruslana. I get the impression that this ominous meeting was just an excuse to get the hyper-motivated bartering reporter out of the dressing room. My mood drops. How could I get myself into such a ridiculous deal? Secret trade meetup at eleven o'clock by the Vudybichi subway station under the three highway overpasses on the edge of the city? Maybe the pop star was just playing a bad joke on me? I can't find an answer, partly because the trucks loudly rattling by keep interrupting my thoughts.

But then I notice a dark limousine with tinted windows slowly driving up to me. The passenger side door opens and Ruslana appears behind big sunglasses. Unbelievable; she kept her promise. After the obligatory left and right kiss, she takes a painting out of the limousine. It is approximately 32 x 20 inches, has a kitschy frame, and an even kitschier motif: a church from Ruslana's hometown. Honestly, the painting could have hung on the brown wallpaper between porcelain angels in my great grandma's hallway circa 1976 and no one would find it out of place. I know that I've agreed to a trade that I can't back out of. I have to take the picture, whether I'm trading up, down, or anywhere else. I react positively to the kitschy picture and give her the wolf painting. Maybe Ruslana realized that I was lying about the wolf? Whatever the case, it is shoved into the limo, Ruslana gives me another kiss, and she hurries off to the airport to keep her appointment with the Kazakh president. I take the kitschy picture back to my apartment and try in vain to acquire a taste for it.

I use the last hours before my flight to visit Peter in Portugal to go to another psychic and get a little motivation for the last seventy days of my trip.

I visit Lilia Romanova on the twenty-third floor of an apartment building. She is a corpulent lady in a mystical psychic outfit (Elvis Presley-style spandex suit with stars on the ends of the sleeves). I ask my question precisely: Will I manage to barter for a house in Hawaii in the next seventy days? Lilia asks her tarot cards and immediately says:

"Sorry, but nothing will come of the house in Hawaii."

Excuse me? Aren't psychics usually paid to give their customers some hope during a crisis, I wonder.

So I ask Lilia to consult her magic pendant. Tarot cards can make mistakes. Lilia swings her pendant and looks at me earnestly:

"If you do get a house, it definitely won't be in Hawaii!"

Now I see how serious she and her fortune-telling tools are about my bad prognosis. I explain that a house anywhere else wouldn't make any sense, since my childhood dream is about Hawaii. After she takes a look in her crystal ball, I ask her to consult her magical metal feather, too. Lilia holds the feather in her hand and waits for it to turn left or right and give her an answer. The magical metal feather is not interested in moving for me. It stays calmly in the middle of her hand. Lilia tells me that this means that 2011 isn't my year and I should try for the house in 2012. Then my time is up and I head to the airport in frustration to catch my flight to Lisbon.

13

BARTERING BY A THREAD

Portugal

Peter is a seventy-two-year-old wealthy and eccentric man, who tells me unbelievable stories about his life.

In the sixties he decided to backpack through Europe. On the way, he and his guitar came to the outskirts of Lisbon, which housed *the* hotel in the country was; all the kings of the world stayed there. The then-twenty-year-old liked that, and he decided to spend some time nearby. It just so happened that young Peter, who was certainly an attractive man, met the sister of a European king on the beach. One thing led to another and the king's sister began to bring him to parties and receptions where she introduced him as Count Peter for fun. And that was the reason why the owner of the hotel offered to let "Count" Peter live in the hotel free of charge, since he of course liked to welcome nobility. So "Count" Peter moved in. One day he was sitting in the lobby when an industry couple went by him and the lady tripped. Count Peter politely helped her to collect all the scattered bits and bobs from her purse, which began a friendship between him and the couple. Peter introduced them to the hotel owner, who he maintained a good relationship with, aided by his supposed noble status. Because of this acquaintance, the couple was able to make a business deal with the hotel owner. As thanks to Peter for introducing them, he got a shoebox. The contents were pretty notable for the sixties: 180,000 Deutschmarks in small bills. Now Count Peter could officially move into the hotel and pay for his expenses out of the shoebox under his bed. These four years were anything but petty bourgeois: meeting pretty, wealthy, and even noble women, excellent contacts, and a jet set life that couldn't be better. So it's no wonder that the mother of his daughter is a former model.

The reason I believe it all: I'm looking at the photos from these stories. Count Peter arm in arm with the model, Count Peter with a European royal family, and so on and so forth. I find myself in the house of a wealthy, cosmopolitan bon vivant who is giving me a glimpse into his life. He tells me that at the moment he has invested a large amount in a company that searches for treasure and is currently bringing up Chinese porcelain with a big machine from a ship that sank off the coast of Borneo during a storm in the fifteenth century. Because of this, Peter's estate is full of "treasures." I've landed here by the best trade partner of my trip, I think, and prepare myself for the best barter of my life.

So I talk to him a little about bartering. This topic reminds him that his father once made a trade in the Second World War. A woman lived with his family and worked as their housekeeper in exchange. Wars are certainly times when bartering blossoms. There are currently thirty wars and conflicts in the word, and it is right in these tragic times that bartering occurs most, Peter says. Money can often be unreliable, and people can often only ensure their survival by trading. I haven't yet thought about the relationship between war and barter, but it's true.

After chatting, we come to the bartering conversation. I show Peter a small treasure chest with a DVD lying on purple silk. Peter wonders what I could have brought him. He asks me to put in the DVD for him. So we sit in front of the computer and watch as Ina and Marina greet Peter and show him around Vinnitsa, all while breathing "Peter" seductively into the microphone. Peter likes this little gag. I'm waiting impatiently for him to offer something in return. I wait, but nothing happens. Finally, I politely ask him what he's putting in.

Peter goes through the packed living room where there are all sorts of antiques and valuable items. He takes a Bible out of the cabinet and offers it to me. This Bible clearly could be worth a lot, but I already have the three-hundred-year-old one and I find it hard to trade antique books. So I have to pass, but not without worrying that I'm going to scare off my trade partner.

I argue that the video is very personal and that it took a lot of work to make it, carefully implying that I'm looking for something more valuable. Peter is somewhat distant. Finally he offers me an old map. But as much as I would like to take it, I was expecting more. I push my luck a little:

"Thank you for that great offer, but I have to say no; I just need something more if I'm going to reach my goal. Maybe we should call the whole thing off."

A silence fills the room, making us both feel uncomfortable. I know that with this statement, I've left myself with nothing. To have flown to Portugal without bartering would be one of the biggest defeats of my trip so far. But then Peter asks if I have anything else to offer. I get the painting from Ruslana, which has been standing in the hallway of his house since I arrived. I tell him the story of the secret trade under the overpass and I tell him that Ruslana is a very famous pop star in Europe. The story excites him.

Then, my salvation: he offers me an antique ivory sundial from the eighteenth century. This sundial was recently valued at over $3,000 by Sotheby's in London. Crazy! I'm extremely happy and almost hug him. Painting and video for an antique clock; it's a perfect deal.

14

LEDERHOSEN AND FOLK MUSIC UNDER THE PALM TREES

Brazil

It's time to head to Rio de Janeiro with the antique clock, the antique Bible, the Torah, and the travel voucher in my luggage. I step onto my next continent just as I had resolved to. It's a place that couldn't be any prettier at first glance: Copacabana, Ipanema, sun, Sugarloaf, attractive people, et cetera. I walk along the beaches, take a cable car up the Sugarloaf, and throw myself into the nightlife. Naturally, I go to a baile funk party. Baile funk is a Brazilian form of hip hop that comes from the favelas, the poor areas of the city. The lyrics often reference the violent realities of life there and the rhythmic music keeps me dancing all night long.

The next morning my hangover announces itself when I wake up with the travel voucher, clock, and religious books next to me. I write the day off. The caipirinhas have given me an unbelievable headache. I take a walk through the city and realize that I have no way to trade in this situation without knowing Portuguese. I collapse onto bed, and there I decide to travel to a city that might not be so radiant at first sight, but promises order, peace, and security: Pomerode!

Pomerode is in southern Brazil and was founded in 1860 by German settlers from northern German Pomerania. Because the German city of Pomerode hasn't had any contact with the German "mothership" in a long time, the Pomeranian culture of the nineteenth century has been preserved and hasn't changed much. The city of twenty-three thousand seems like it is sunken in a fairytale sleep. Almost all the residents are of German descent and hold on to their cultural roots. Many live in timber frame houses and some even wear German Trachten (Lederhosen and Dirndls); there are sixteen active shooting clubs and six folk dancing groups. And the city apparently has the highest beer consumption per capita in Brazil.

In Pomerode, people speak and write Pommersch. Since the people emigrated, the language developed independently from German and it sounds pretty funny to me.

I check into the Hotel Schroeder. Its German surname is not particularly striking, since next door is Krause Realty, and a little bit further down is the house of the Wege family. I describe my mission to the very competent lady at the tourism office and show her my bartering goods. She offers to consult with the vice mayor because she likes that someone from Germany wants to trade with people in Pomerode. A little later she tells me that the vice mayor also thinks my project is exciting, and they ask that I create a little exhibition with my computer and projector.

The Bartering Dream in Bartering Mecca

I get started right away. I print posters advertising a lecture in the town hall. On the posters along with the title "Wigge's Barter for Paradise," there are photos from Africa, Australia, and other scenes of the trip so far. When I'm hanging the posters up, I already have the first few curious locals coming up to me and getting excited that someone from Germany is making a presentation. A little later Ivone, who works in the tourism office, tells me that the German language, folk music-heavy radio station would like to do an interview with me about the trip. Shortly after, I'm speaking to all of Pomerode, calling for the listeners to come to my exhibition in the town hall (Preifektura). This seems to help.

Two days later, the town hall fills with residents of the city, all excited about bartering. Some are dressed in traditional Trachten. And then I give an almost hour-long illustrated talk about my trip and all the adventures that have come along with it.

Everyone is excited, and I get three (!) trade offers right after the talk. Christian, who is dressed in Lederhosen and works as an auto mechanic, offers me a potential trade for his VW bug. I take down his number. Then I hear from Claudio, who works in the Pomerode zoo and suggests that he might be able to find one animal he could offer in trade. I note his number, too. Then the barter-happy vice mayor comes up to me and suggests that the community all together could put up a bigger trade. I'm blown away by all the offers. I haven't had this much interest in the whole trip up until now combined.

The next day, I take my items to the zoo. Elephants, giraffes, and an anteater greet the bartering reporter. I'm immediately interested in the anteater, since they only live in South America. Its long tubular snout and the even longer tongue are just too funny.

I meet Claudio and immediately ask if we could think about an anteater trade. Claudio laughs. Instead of answering, he takes me to the anteater habitat. A fully grown anteater comes running toward me in excitement, but a zookeeper immediately holds it away from me with a loop on a long metal rod. I don't understand why there has to be such a fuss. Claudio explains that anteaters have three-inch claws that they use to fight. They can even kill people with them. I realize that an anteater trade probably won't happen. We leave the habitat and I see the anteater coming toward me again, but this time I avoid any further contact.

We talk about animals and which ones could be considered for a trade. Claudio suggests a parrot that is acclimated to humans and can be easily transported. I agree and show him my items for trade: the voucher is too valuable, the clock is too niche, and he can't quite relate to the five books of Moses, so he takes the three-hundred-year-old Bible. I leave the zoo. Claudio will bring the parrot to me at Hotel Schroeder the next day.

To the delight of the other hotel guests, the bird is delivered and handed over to me. It is colorful, as parrots are, but it doesn't want to repeat any of the funny things I say to it. So I sit in my room, with the parrot sitting silently next to me. What now? A bird is sitting here, so what do I do? Maybe it's thirsty? I get it a bowl of water and watch as it ignores it. Apparently drinking isn't so important. Does it want to play? I try to play with it, but it isn't interested in me.

I realize that a bird is a difficult thing and that I can't be responsible for it. In panic, I get a piece of bread from the hotel kitchen, even though I have no idea if parrots eat that.

On the way back to my room, I meet a maid who starts to laugh hysterically and hides behind me, probably because she doesn't want to be filmed or maybe because she finds it hilarious for someone to be filming themselves while getting food. I try to calm her down, but she can't stop laughing. Every time I try to turn toward her, she turns with me, so that she is permanently giggling behind my back. While I try to calm the camera-shy maid, I see the parrot sneak out of the room and waddle across the hall to another maid. A little bit later I find him sitting peacefully on her arm. It's official: the bird just doesn't like me!

I have to do something. First, I bring the parrot back to the zoo where they can take care of him. In the meantime, I meet Christian, who had offered to trade the VW bug at the town hall. He doesn't think the parrot is a very attractive offer, but then his wife pipes up, saying that she instantly fell in love with the bird.

So we discuss the trade in detail. Bird for car? The parrot would actually not be very cheap to buy from an exotic pet store. But Christian, dressed very traditionally in Lederhosen, explains that even his oldest VW bug from 1966 is worth 4,000 real, or 2,000 euros. So I offer him a deal: Christian and I will race. He'll race one hundred meters in his old VW bug, and I'll ride on an old bicycle with a thirty-meter head start. If he wins, we won't trade, but if I win, we trade the bird for the VW. Christian seems to have a good sense of humor, and he agrees to the race.

We stand on a gravel road outside Pomerode, it's humid and warm, and every movement causes an outbreak of sweat. These aren't the best conditions for winning a race against a car with an old bicycle with no gear shift. Christian revs his engine thirty meters behind me. He also puts on the parking brake, takes it off, and puts it on again. The bug bounces after me amid loud shouting.

But then Ivone from the tourism office gives us the signal. On your marks, get set, go!

I push on the pedals, but because of the missing gear shift, I don't make much progress. Luckily, Christian's bug doesn't accelerate quickly, so after fifty meters he is still behind me. But then it gets close. Christian drives right up to me and tries to pass me on the left. But the bicycle is swinging from left to right because I am pedaling while standing. It makes it impossible for Christian to pass me. It wasn't my intention, but maybe it should just be filed under "luck." At the finish line, Christian is still just behind me; he failed to pass me. The exchange is perfect. Christian admits defeat and hands over the bug. He'll pick up the parrot at the zoo later.

After already having traded for a riding mower and a broken down tuk-tuk, I am now the proud owner of a car. I've been wanting a car for so long on this trip, and I finally have it—old, but drivable and in one piece. I drive the rattling bug proudly through Pomerode, past timber frame houses and historical churches that would have fit right in provincial Germany.

The VW bug, antique clock from 1750, and a travel voucher together are worth over $16,000; still far from the price of a house, but a 16,000 fold increase from the apple. However, I want to go to New York next, and imagining driving the bug there is beyond idealistic. It's clear that no matter how nice the car is, I have to trade it quickly. But I still have an ace up my sleeve: the vice mayor talked about a trade with the whole community.

I meet her and tell her that I'm incredibly proud of the bug, but it unfortunately has to stay in Pomerode. The vice mayor understands my situation. She tells me that she could arrange a trade with the local porcelain manufacturer Schmidt, if I can give her the bug. I'm cautious because I definitely don't want to trade for something of lesser value. I tell her that the bug is worth at least 4,000 real. She nods and tells me that a twelve-piece table set from this manufacturer can cost up to 8,000 real.

The next day, Ivone from the tourism office takes me to the porcelain manufacturer. She is in charge of arranging the trade for the vice mayor. We stand in the factory showroom, where the porcelain sets are displayed in cases. I see expensive, cheap, beautiful, and kitschy sets—everything that the porcelain-loving heart could desire. We discuss which set I can have with the boss. After a brief discussion with the owner, Ivone makes a suggestion. She suggests a game. I get exactly thirty seconds to choose a set from the display cases in the showroom. Since all the sets are displayed without any price tag, it becomes a game of luck. If I choose a cheap set, I've lost value drastically, but if I choose an expensive one, it could be the best trade of the whole trip. I debate whether I should take the offer, but what other alternative do I have? I have to travel to the US soon for my bartering blitz finale. I'm simply running out of time, so I agree.

Ivone gives me the start signal yet again. I run back and forth through the showroom cases like a crazy person. I almost take a tumble, which would be disastrous considering there are valuables worth thousands all around me. But it's all okay, and I inspect the saucers and cups like the wind.

How can you tell the worth of a china set? I approach it pragmatically: everything white is out, since it looks somehow uncreative; everything with bright colors too, since it reminds me of IKEA porcelain. So I concentrate on plates and cups that have gold decorations. Customers that buy things like that have money, I think, and at second thirty, I decide on a set with a squiggly gold design.

I stand right before the resolution of the puzzle. I'm really flustered. Is it an 8,000 or 80,000 real set? The company owner takes a price tag out of a big box that contains the complete service. I see twelve little cups, twelve big cups, twelve plates, twelve little saucers, twelve big saucers, a bowl, a coffee pot, a big pot, a milk pitcher, and a sugar bowl, all made from the best porcelain.

But what is it all worth? I watch the boss slowly turn the tag over in his hand. Lots of thoughts are running through my head, among others, what would happen if it were a dud? Should I undo it all or disappear from the factory and jump into the bug like James Bond, to drive to New York? No! I agreed to this game and I must accept what comes. Then I read the number on the price tag: 5,000–6,000 real, negotiable.

I am relieved. Even if I count on the lower price, it's still 1,000 real more than the bug was worth. A weight falls from my shoulders and I hand the key to the bug to Ivone, so it can stay in Pomerode. I think this is a successful closing, but then the phone rings. It's a certain Ronald, who wants to make a trade with me. He tells me that he is the son of a German immigrant who has lived in São Paulo for years. But now he wants to have an idyllic and especially a secure life with his family in Pomerode. He tells me that his life in the huge metropolis São Paulo was unbelievably dangerous. Accidents and even murders were not rare in his former neighborhood.

I meet him in his country house and tell him that the porcelain, travel voucher, and antique clock have a high value and that I want to invest as little as possible, so that I can keep my house in Hawaii goal in my sight. Ronald understands my position, but then he shows me his trade item: its name is Hansi, it has four legs, and one day it will grow up to be a proud stallion—it's a young pony. Hansi looks perfectly ludicrous as he stares at me questioningly. He is a strange and living trade item.

But soon we figure out that Ronald can't do anything with the clock or the voucher, and also has enough porcelain already. So I offer my labor: cleaning the barn, grooming horses, etc. He doesn't seem to trust my qualifications as a stable boy, and says he would rather do it himself.

So we sit across from each other for a moment in silence, until I suddenly remember that I also have the Torah in my backpack, which the Jewish synagogue in Ukraine traded for the book from the Orthodox convent. I'm sure it won't interest him, but I'm wrong. He finds the trade very attractive and would love to read the Torah.

It's hard to believe, but Ronald really trades his pony for the five books of Moses. I ask what his motive is for this generous trade, which really doesn't have many material benefits for him. He explains that at the moment, he has too many newborn ponies and so it's not a problem to trade one of them. We go out to the field to fetch Hansi. Sounds easy enough—you just climb over a fence, put a harness on him, and then you're out again. It would be that simple if Hansi was tamed. I learn again that animal trades should be fully thought through. The items for barter are living creatures with their own opinions about the trade. The next thirty minutes go as follows:

I walk up to Hansi, Hansi walks away; I run after Hansi with a lasso, he hides behind the big horses; I run toward them, the whole gang runs away, I run panting after them, slip in the wet mud, pull myself up, run again, and manage to separate Hansi from the herd and trap him in a corner. I throw the lasso, Hansi bucks and runs underneath it, I run to the other side of the field, and I'm totally out of breath. Hansi, of course, is back on the other side. I throw the lasso around aimlessly and the herd sighs, "How ridiculous." I approach Hansi again; Hansi feigns to the left, but then goes right, I almost fall again, and then I repeat the whole thing over again.

Then Ronald opens the pasture door so that Hansi and the other ponies can walk into the barn, where it's a dead end. I throw the lasso and Hansi is mine. But Hansi doesn't want to walk behind me on the rope. He pulls, plants himself in one spot, and then takes off suddenly.

I know that this wild pony needs to go even faster than the parrot. So I consult with Ronald about whether he could find another trade partner who wants the pony today. He gives me the names of two people who own pony stables in the city, and I call them right away. The first declines; he has no need right now. The second is named Addulah and happens to be looking for a pony.

So Hansi is loaded into Roland's trailer and before long we're at Addulah's stable. He is in his mid-forties and rents out little timber frame bungalows to tourists who can then ride his ponies or horses. He likes Hansi and Hansi likes the other ponies. But will Addulah barter with me?

Addulah ponders what he has. He offers me two watches. I can't judge their value, so I turn them down. Then he offers me a Brazilian soccer uniform, which won't be very appealing to the soccer haters in the US. Finally, we agree that he will give me a smart phone for the pony, since that will be tradable in any country. I happily leave Pomerode with a travel voucher, an antique clock, a porcelain set, and a smart phone.

But my good luck ends at the airport. The box of porcelain weighs over forty pounds, so I can't carry it on. At the counter, I argue that the porcelain is expensive and breakable, but it does no good, so I get big plastic bags and stuff them full of scrunched up newspaper. I stick the carton into the thickly padded bag so that the good porcelain is at least a little bit protected. It looks funny. A big ball goes down the luggage belt. As I board the plane, my uneasy feeling is justified. I see an airport worker toss the big paper ball with the porcelain onto a truck, despite the "fragile" warning sticker. I could burst, especially because the ladies at the counter repeatedly assured me that no one would handle the porcelain carelessly. The flight to New York is pretty frustrating because I can't check if my porcelain is still in one piece.

My salvation is on the luggage claim at John F. Kennedy Airport. To the amusement of the other guests, the big paper ball comes down the conveyor belt. The porcelain was not damaged. I got all my things to the US in one piece!

15

A MICROCOSM OF THE WORLD

USA

New York: with over eight million people, a multicultural population, and a mentality that, as I understand it, is pretty open to crazy actions, may be the perfect place for my bartering finale. Many here find the idea of bartering from an apple to a house to be pretty funny. Once I arrive, I am also very confident that my finale in the US will be a success because my good experiences in the bartering Mecca of Pomerode continue to have a good effect.

In order to be really well prepared, I again think of a list of alternative uses for my newest item, the porcelain. And as a serious trade partner, I always want to make sure that what I think of will really function in the real world. So I go up to the flat roof of my Brooklyn hostel and test the following usage options for a porcelain service:

Plate as flying saucer: perfect for when you want to prove the existence of extraterrestrials to your friends.

Porcelain as a projectile during a fight with your significant other: useful for emotionally loaded situations.

Plate as Frisbee: even I am surprised at how well the plates can fly.

Cup as tool to measure the height of a building: you only have to drop the cup from the roof of the building you want to measure. You can measure the exact height by the length of the fall.

Plates as building blocks: with a little delicacy and ten stacked plates, you can build the leaning tower of Pisa. Ten is the limit, otherwise the tower starts leaning too much.

Since all of the attempts at alternative uses for a porcelain service can only be attempted once, I was happy to have found a cheap porcelain set in the store on the corner. The test service is completely destroyed by the end, but I proved that all of the above uses function excellently.

Armed with new arguments and packed with my trade items, I ride into Manhattan every day to bring the things to the people.

Manhattan totally overwhelms me. The countless skyscrapers, the fast tempo of the people; every corner seems to be different from the previous one. It's Little Italy, then SoHo, Central Park, Wall Street, Broadway, East Village, et cetera. On this island that composes the central borough of New York City, you can see the entire world go by in fast forward. But which corner is the friendliest for bartering?

I decide on Wall Street. Lots of rich people must walk around here, thinking all day about trading. Wouldn't the brokers and investors have the desire to trade something concrete after a long day of working with abstract numbers? An antique clock, for example, or a travel voucher?

My first attempts prove to be difficult because it's mostly just crowds of tourists flowing by me with each minute. They respond to me in Chinese or Italian and usually have nothing more to offer than a recently bought postcard.

But then I meet Barry, an American in his fifties, who is interested in my project because he himself likes to barter. He tells me that a little while ago, he owed money to his wireless provider. He called up the hotline and offered to sing a song to the person in charge of his account. Unbelievable, but the deal worked: Barry sang her a song and the debt was forgotten.

I'm impressed that such an unconventional trade is possible in our commercial world, especially in the US. Barry says that he could offer something very special for one of my items. He tells me that he used to work for a radio station near Chicago and that when he was cleaning out the archives, he found some original Beatles interviews on audio tape that had never been heard before. Wow, what a trade!

I immediately imagine myself trading this unique item with a Beatles fan club for a house in Hawaii. But unfortunately, Barry quickly tears me away from my fantasies when he suddenly proclaims that he will never give up the tapes. So I continue on down Wall Street unsuccessfully, and finally end my search for the day due to heavy rain; I'm soaking wet.

I continue on Wall Street the next day, but one no becomes two, then four, then eight, then sixteen, thirty-two. I give up at the sixty-fourth no when it becomes clear to me that Wall Street is too concerned with money and my offer is too unconventional for many people. So I move on through Manhattan and end up standing at West 4th street.

Here, in the middle of the city, is one of the most famous basketball courts for amateurs. It's lovingly known as The Cage because the court is surrounded by fences. The people here are all good, tall, mostly African American players who play hard.

Since I used to play at least halfway decently, I get excited about a game. Could I challenge one of these players to a match and get something new in trade if I win? I talk to the shortest of all the players. His name is Dexter, he is strongly built, and he's only 5'6", six inches shorter than me. I invite him to play a little game; whoever gets three points first wins. If he wins, he can have my smart phone from Pomerode. If I win, I get a laptop from him.

Dexter consults his friends about this unusual offer. I hear the other players, who used to play in the East Coast League or as pros in Europe, warn him. One advises him to be careful, since such a confident offer could only come from a pro. But Dexter agrees, and the ball is thrown up in the air between us.

Three seconds later it's 1:0 for Dexter, and I haven't even touched the ball once. The ball is tossed up again, and I hit it and excitedly dribble to the left down the court. But just another three seconds later and it's 2:0. The ball is tossed up a third time. Before I can even react, it's 3:0 for Dexter, and the total play time has been thirty seconds.

What a crazy idea! To challenge a West 4th street player, even if he is only 5'6", is total basketball suicide. A grinning Dexter receives the smart phone, and I leave the court frustrated and plagued by worry about what will happen next.

If bartering on the street doesn't work, I'll go back to a strategy that I tried in Germany: the big media offensive.

After all, my story is exciting. Why wouldn't the American media jump on a story about a German trying to turn an apple into a Hawaiian dream house? So cameraman Jakob and I contact at least a hundred representatives of TV shows, radio programs, and newspapers. We say the same thing to all of them:

"Hello, Barterman is in the city and is searching for a trade partner. Would it be possible to advertise for him on your show, or on the front page of your paper?"

A few media representatives signal at least some interest; others decline immediately. It is also quite a problem to get any editors on the phone. Either you get a voicemail asking you to leave a message, or you are forwarded to another voicemail by someone in the wrong department. It's always the same game. Pretty much no one calls back. It's a shame; I could so easily imagine myself popping up in a New York newspaper.

As a precaution, I also write to ten friends and acquaintances in the US, offering to barter with them. That produces a further twenty-five contacts, but still no concrete offers. And like before, I post calls for trades on various online platforms, but it doesn't bring in anything quickly.

Barterman!

I clearly need to improve on my "American media offensive" strategy, so I spontaneously decide to buy myself a Flash costume. I alter the red, skintight bodysuit by putting a big Barterman sticker on the chest, and cut into the hood to remove the colored stripes—The Flash becomes the still unknown Barterman!

I ride back to Manhattan with my new identity. The people on the subway cheer for me—New Yorkers like their superheroes. Many seem to wonder, which superhero is that, anyway? I'm too red for Batman, don't have the spider pattern for Spiderman, and Superman definitely doesn't have red fringe on his forehead. So I point to the sticker on my chest, and many people appear to enjoy the expansions of the super-hero family.

As I walk among the skyscrapers, I let the passersby know that Barterman has a serious need to barter. Many people ask about it, want to know all the details, promise to tell their friends about Barterman, and take little cards from me which read: YOU WANT TO BARTER WITH BARTERMAN? CONTACT ME AT GERMANBARTERMAN@GMAIL.COM!

I have a good feeling about this strategy. It seems to amuse the New Yorkers. In my enthusiasm, I do some crazy stunts on the city streets, documenting Barterman's selfless mission for the residents of New York. First, I kick start a moving taxi, and then carry a perfectly capable young woman across the street. Barterman has hardly finished this deed when he runs across the street and demonstrates his athleticism with a successful somersault.

I finally give away all of my business cards, but I have to wait for any success. The next day, I still haven't gotten an email.

Nature Strikes Back

In the meantime, my stress is growing; a week in New York, four fruitless campaigns, and a gambled away smart phone. And there is more bad news: there is an earthquake near New York that measuring five to six on the Richter scale. It shakes and quakes in New York, and luckily, nothing else happens, but this ends up having big consequences for me. When I try to make further media contacts, they all tell me that all the news is about the earthquake right now.

Then the news comes in that Hurricane Irene will be hitting New York in a few days. Hurricanes, like earthquakes, rarely occur on the east coast, so New York prepares for the worst. Entire neighborhoods near the Hudson River are evacuated because of expected flooding. This weather forecast makes it totally impossible to pitch Baterman to the media; they would much rather have Superman.

Several bleak days go by, and I'm in quite a jam. Thousands of New Yorkers are evacuating, windows are barred, and businesses are closed.

But the bars in Brooklyn are wide open. They're full to the brim just hours before the storm is supposed to hit. The people inside all toast to a "Happy Hurricane," but even Barterman feels a little uneasy at the forecasted 90-mile-per-hour winds. Perhaps the Brooklynites have the right idea, I think, so I drink to a "Happy Hurricane" with them. At about one in the morning, the storm gets so strong that I can hardly get back to my apartment, while behind me I still hear "Rock Me like a Hurricane" blaring from the bar.

There is good news the next morning. We didn't get hit with the worst, but the streets are still a mess. And then there is good news for the bartering scene, too. My friend Sayuri, who had already helped arrange the gold trade with billionaire Jim Rogers, contacts me. She says that the Danish artist Marianne Engberg, who lives in Brooklyn, would like to barter with me.

I visit this renowned artist who dedicates herself to pinhole photography. Her pictures reach back to the older form of photography where the artists take pictures of objects with their pinhole cameras. The result is flat but very highly focused images that look like drawings. In the last several decades, Marianne Engberg has made a name for herself with her photos, not just in New York, but on the international art scene as well.

She gets right down to business: she needs a promotional video for her recently published biography. Sure, no problem, the cameramen Jakob and Dominik and I already did that for the yogi Panta in India. In return, Marianne offers me something very special; she says that in 1972, she received a mission from the art god Salvador Dali. He appeared in her studio one morning and asked her to expose a thousand beans with the image of Mao Tse-tung. Then the beans should be given out in New York as a political and artistic statement. So Marianne exposed a picture of Mao's face on tiny beans. It was not actually a thousand beans, since the project was ended early. Then all the beans were given out in New York.

The only thing that remains of this project today is a black and white photo that portrays the art project and Marianne wants to trade this photo for the video. I am excited by the story and agree right away, even before Marianne mentions that the gallery price of this unique print would be about $5,000.

It's a done deal. I will shoot a video about Marianne's life work, and I will get the Dali-Engberg-Mao photo, which I personally like quite a lot. However, I am upset that future trade partners won't really know the worth of this unique print.

With this successful trade, my mission in New York is fulfilled, and I prepare to fly to the west coast. As I stow all my trade items on the plane, I think of the travel voucher that I've had since Africa and which became an unexpected shelf warmer. As I wonder if I can get rid of it in the US, it occurs to me that it is unclear whether Hilde would pay for the much longer flight from the States to Tanzania—we never discussed my giving the voucher to anyone outside Germany. I decide to call Hilde.

As I feared, she says that two tickets to Tanzania from America would totally throw off her calculations, and she can't really finance that. We debate what we could do, until Hilde gets the idea to trade back, since she still wants to support my bartering blitz. At first I hesitate, since it is a financial loss for me. But finally, I take the offer; it is very generous despite everything. Gold has a much more certain value and is a popular thing to trade because of that.

When the three ounces of gold arrive to me in San Francisco by mail a day later, I toss the travel voucher away. I immediately look up the current price of gold and find that the trade-back wasn't so bad after all. While the price of gold in May, (when I got the coins from Jim Rogers) was $1,500 per ounce, it has risen to $1,900. So the value of the three ounces of gold has risen from $4,500 to $5,700!

Giving vs. Trading

In San Francisco, I immediately begin a new media offensive to finally trade all my possessions.

Once again, there are a lot of phone calls and not much response, even though this time there is no natural disaster standing in the way of Barterman coverage. So that I'm not just waiting for responses without doing anything, I decide to make a side trip to Nevada, where the annual Burning Man Festival is being held.

Apart from the fact that the festival must be an unbelievably shocking event (fifty thousand people to gather in the middle of nowhere), I also heard that the visitors love bartering. For a week, a sort of artificial city is erected in the Black Rock Desert in Nevada with the help of all the participants. At the end of it, the entire city vanishes without a trace.

I can't remember ever having been at a crazier and more exciting festival: many of the visitors wear eccentric clothing, paint their bodies, or are naked. Everyone takes part in the creative development of the imaginary city that exists during the festival. For example, the visitors build their own vehicles in which they move across the huge expanse. I see a giant UFO with people dancing on it to electro beats, an indescribable fellow who looks like he came straight from the movie *Water World*, futuristically made-over bicycles, and golf carts that look like they came from another planet. Then there are people dancing again on huge trucks made to look like Noah's ark. The scenery is full of fantasy and creativity and is totally overwhelming.

At the climax of the event, a huge figure of a man is burned. This ritual has existed since 1986, when Larry Harvey and some friends burned an eight-foot wooden figure of a man in honor of the summer solstice. This idea was continuously developed, and twenty-five years later, the dimensions are very different: on Friday evening after sunset, a sixty-five-foot Trojan horse is burned before forty thousand silent watchers. On Saturday evening, an eight-foot man suffers the same fate, and on Sunday, it is a huge wooden temple, one hundred feet tall and one hundred and sixty-five feet across. The mood in the moments when art is burned is unbelievable. It all happens in total silence; no one yells or fools around. There is overwhelming respect and awe—it's indescribable!

I meet David. He is about fifty, and stands with a big tuba in the middle of the desert playing music. For this scene, that would be normal, but with every note that David blows from his tuba, fire shoots up out of the instrument. While he plays, another man joins him, playing the trumpet. Finally, there is a half-naked woman playing a balloon as a horn by letting the air out slowly. The trio is quickly surrounded by people who applaud and sing along.

Later, I talk to David and find out that he is the director of *The Simpsons* and is the one who decided that Lisa Simpson should play the cartoon saxophone. I ask him if he would like to barter with me, since I heard that that is a part of the festival, so to speak. But David explains that I understood wrong. It is true, that people bring things with them, but they bring them to give them away without getting anything in return.

And it's true; I see someone giving away hundreds of hot dogs, someone else cooking bacon on the hood of his car and giving it away, and someone else giving out sun block.

Yes, I am disappointed, because this isn't a place to barter. But my excitement is bigger than my disappointment. It's unbelievable that all these people come together in the desert to simply give each other gifts and create a warm, happy atmosphere.

Okay, bartering-wise, nothing else is going to happen here, I get that. But maybe there is a soothsayer here among all the crazy people, who can give me a bit of courage for the last forty days of my mission. I meet Nathalie-Eva and her boyfriend, who are both dressed in feathers and leather clothing and look like some kind of Indian shamans. They're celebrating wildly, and they tell me that they can definitely see a little into the future at this moment. And they immediately have an answer to my burning question:

"Yeah, it's going to work out with the house! Don't worry, just party with us!"

It remains to be seen how much of this statement contains true psychic qualities, but anyway, I paint my whole body with gold paint, put on some red sunglasses and a green headdress to complete my Martian look, and throw myself into the tumult.

After a lot of partying, I'm on my way back to my tent when a young Australian asks if he can give me his BMX bike; he has to fly home tonight. I'm astounded at this natural joy for giving, and before I can offer to trade something, he is already racing away in his camper. And that's not all. Later in the day I find a beach cruiser, one of those retro sixties bikes, in front of my tent. There is a sign on it: BIKE AS GIFT! An anonymous giver had simply left it there. Somehow I begin to wonder how far this will all go. Will they give me that Noah's ark that drives by my tent regularly with hundreds of partiers on it?

To take part in the gift-giving culture, I give beer and water to other festival-goers, and then I happen to meet someone interested in trading. A young woman would like to trade her BMX for my golden beach cruiser. I'm in, since the beach cruiser won't really fit in my car.

Barterman on American TV

On the way back to San Francisco, I think a lot about the festival. It was a very important experience. Bartering is really cool, but giving is much more fun! I somehow have the feeling that I have to pay it forward after receiving such generous gifts. At any rate, I know that I will come back the next year with many gifts packed.

As lovely as the giving was, I have another assignment at the moment. Back in San Francisco, I devote myself to my bartering campaign again. Before the festival, I informed the local media that at one o'clock in the afternoon today, I would be performing a very special stunt at the tallest building in the city in "the world famous barter blanket" (the warmth and love blanket from TK). I had hoped that this message would attract droves of reporters, but no matter how much I jump around in front of the building in the "barter blanket" and do warm-ups for a not-entirely-thought-out stunt, the only people I meet are German tourists. Not one reporter showed up for the appointment! So I leave the pathetic stage.

When I'm back at the hostel, another email comes in. Jeannie Lynch, a journalist from ABC Radio, apologizes that she couldn't make it to the great barter blanket stunt and invites me to come to the radio station in downtown San Francisco wearing the Barterman costume. On the radio? Obviously she wants to have some fun. The interview is aired live, and as usual, I send my pleas to barter to the listening audience.

An editor from Comcast TV Network writes to me. She asks if I would like to be on a prime time talk show with host Dave Benz to present all my trade items live. I'm completely over the moon—this could be the breakthrough for the bartering blitz. I decide to use the power of the Barterman costume on this program, too.

Sitting there in my mask, I'm surprised no one in the audience is surprised to see me in a skintight red costume with fringe on my head. Quite the opposite, they seem to have all expected just that. Dave is a typical American host in a suit with a pretentious comment about everything and everyone. First he chats about sports, particularly football and baseball, and interviews professional athletes until it's finally time:

"And now let's welcome Michael Wigge from Germany, who is traveling through America as Barterman!"

Dave just can't get enough of the story and he bombards me with questions. He's incredibly excited about the red-suited Barterman in the chair across from him. I'm allowed to display a 30 x 8-inch sign on the table with my email address so that every Californian has the chance to trade with Barterman. At the end of the interview, he offers me a trade. He holds up a Starbucks gift card that he found that morning. He explains that he doesn't know how much is on the card—maybe nothing, maybe a million dollars. Dave offers it to me, and in exchange I have to do the chicken dance. I immediately agree, but I crack under pressure and can't remember what the chicken dance is. In my panic, I perform a Russian cossack dance instead. My faux pas doesn't seem to be too serious, since Dave laughs and lets me have the card (which bought me all of two coffees).

Now the bleak days of waiting begin again. I was certain that my email account would be blowing up after this TV appearance, but it isn't. I get one offer from a Markus, but he doesn't pick up his phone. If such a sensational TV appearance doesn't help, what will?

Doubt creeps in again. How am I going to do this? I'm scared that I miscalculated my success. I was so certain that appearing in the American media was the sure way to victory.

I begin to earnestly think about simply trading for wood in Hawaii and building a house myself or just squatting in some abandoned shed. But then I shake all the dark thoughts out of my head and look forward, toward LA.

Hollywood

I drive down Highway 101 toward Los Angeles, passing endless houses, highways, and cars. Frightening . . . I don't know where I should turn, so I reach out to my home base and contact Sayuri and Sabine again, the two friends who helped me in India and Singapore. Sabine contacts me a day later and gives me a name: Ariane Sommer, former German TV host, Hollywood reporter for the tabloid *Gala*, author, blonde, and someone who knows every Tom, Dick, and Harry in LA.

We meet in Beverly Hills and Ariane tells me about her contacts, who range from show business people to rich businessmen. She spontaneously calls up a few rich and famous people to get them excited about bartering, but she either gets voicemail or is told that the person has no time.

She has more luck with Jessica, who runs a Porsche store in Beverly Hills. Jessica is also German and thinks the bartering blitz is totally "amazing," which is the positive reaction I had expected from Americans. We go to the car dealership and I show Jessica the Salvador Dali/ Engberg art. She is unfortunately not very excited about the photo. I offer the antique clock, and Jessica takes the bait. Antiques always do well in the US, maybe because the country's history doesn't reach very far back.

Jessica agrees to a trade. She shows me a pair of pants, apparently a pair of promotional Porsche pants that Ralf Möller, a German bodybuilder and actor, wore. I decline politely. My clock is definitely more valuable than the pants, even if Ralf Möller wore them. Then Jessica shows me a leather motorcycle jacket with a retail value of over $3,000. Now we're in the right price range. But who would wear a thick leather jacket in Hawaii?

I make a suggestion. There is a Porsche clock glinting at me from a display case. A modern luxury clock for a historical sundial sounds pretty good. But Jessica declines this trade with slight annoyance; the clock has a retail value of over $30,000. She leads me to another display case of clocks, pulls out a different model, and offers it in trade. I ask how much it costs, she says $6,400. The deal is done! I give Ariane and Jessica big hugs because this trade nearly doubles the value of my offer. Jessica proudly tells me that she will display the antique clock in the store to remember Barterman.

I call Sabine the second I get back to my hostel to thank her for this connection, and in the meantime, she has gathered even more contacts in Los Angeles. She herself worked in media in Germany for a long time and knows a few Hollywood stars as well as a few who wish they were.

Someone named Jim who is trying to be an actor in LA connects me with Alex Stenzel, a German immigrant whose life story couldn't be any crazier. At the age of sixteen, he was one of the top thirty junior tennis players in the world. At twenty, he was a millionaire with his own fashion label. At twenty-five, he was broke and living in a van under a bridge in Dusseldorf. He had his breakthrough with patent development in Los Angeles.

I meet the forty-something-year-old in his stately house in the LA hills. Alex Stenzel is the embodiment of the American dream: he was prepared to take big risks on his climb to the top, always in danger of falling, always doing his own thing without caring what other people thought or what convention prescribed. Alex is athletic and muscular, has just come from surfing, and wants to head out soon to go rock climbing. He talks without pause, the man is pure energy. Since I can hardly get a word in, I watch what he does. Apparently his home contains five hundred works of art, all by him, photographs, and paintings. And I really, really like the big, painted photographs that are hanging on the walls.

I show Alex Marianne Engberg's photo of the beans that she developed for Salvador Dali. I tell him that this is a very unique piece. Alex likes the offer; he is particularly into Salvador Dali. He wants to trade and even suggests that I choose something from his large collection. I ask about the value of the paintings, and the number eight thousand immediately comes up—dollars of course. His confident demeanor leaves no room to doubt him. Even though I have no objective way to test his claim, I agree to the trade on pragmatic grounds. Somehow my feelings say that I will be better able to trade a big, colorful painting in Hawaii than a small, inconspicuous photograph. I have to speculate that I won't meet any more art connoisseurs, but rather people who will be influenced by visuals. So I agree.

Alex gets an approximately 40 x 30-inch black-and-white photograph from the cabinet, one which he took himself. Then he gets some white and red paint and paints a few lines over the big photo—swoosh, and the art is done in less than five minutes. I am practically frozen. I can hear the number eight thousand being murmured in the background.

I'm astounded. Is it really possible to get $8,000 richer in five minutes like this? To be honest, at moments like these you get the feeling that life isn't always about what you can do, but rather about your confidence. I suddenly wonder if I could have sold my "amateur" crocodile painting that I traded with Diana for $8,000 if only I was confident enough. Maybe I could have even gotten $80,000 for it.

I thank Alex for the piece and ask politely if there is anything else he could add to his offer. Alex seems a little confused. He can probably

hear that I have doubts about the value of his picture, but he charm-
ingly makes a deal with me. He rents out a room in his house for
people who want to visit LA for the weekend. The room costs $398 for
the weekend. He writes me a coupon for a weekend, and we are both
happy with this barter meeting.

Music Star Barterman

It's starting to get crowded in the car. Next to the three ounces of gold
is the big box with the porcelain. On top of that are the two BMX
bikes, taken apart. They are decorated with a Porsche clock and topped
off with Alex's artwork and the coupon. I check my phone during the
drive and see a message from my friend Sayuri, who helped me meet
Jim Rogers and Marianne Engberg.

Sayuri lives in New York and worked in the media there. That's
how she knows everyone, from rich and famous to crazy, creative, and
eccentric, a lot like my friend Sabine from Cologne. Sayuri writes:
"Drive right to Venice Beach this afternoon. A friend of my friend
would like to meet you and possibly barter with you. His name: Coati
Mundi. A bit about him: actor on *Miami Vice*, was with Madonna in
Who's that Girl. Was a top 40 singer in America."

Wow, that sounds great—a Hollywood actor and singer could
be very helpful. I find myself on Venice Beach with Coati, a Puerto
Rican by birth, while skateboarders, cyclists, joggers, and rollerblad-
ers rush by us. Coati is totally in the role of actor. He grimaces and
makes one joke after another. I tell him that I would love to barter
with him, but that I would prefer not to give away any more of the
things I have, because I'm about to go to Hawaii, where I will need
as much as possible. So I show him the warmth and love blanket that
has accompanied me for 175 days. You pull the brown, floppy blanket
over your whole body and just your face sticks out. Your hands are
covered by brown mittens that are sewn onto the blanket. A friend in
Berlin gave it to me before my trip. And then there are also big red
hearts on it. Coati looks at me and asks what that is supposed to be.

I introduce the blanket as the "world-famous barter blanket." Coati has to laugh, but he would have preferred the three ounces of gold or the porcelain set. He pulls a record out of his bag, allegedly a limited edition release that should be worth a lot to Coati Mundi fans. But would I meet those fans in Hawaii? Coati reassures me. He is pretty well-known in the US, but he requests an additional service from me in exchange: I will make music with him on Venice Beach. He'll drum and I'll wear dog paw mittens and sing the following lyrics on a loop: I – Love – My – Dog!

I can't sing at all, so I'm nervous. I've never sung a good note in my life and now I'm supposed to sing these absurd lyrics on the beach in front of all these cool people while Coati drums? Okay, okay, it's obviously not about a stellar musical performance—I'm just supposed to be a clown for Coati. Fine then. . . .

I nervously put on the mittens, but Coati is not done. I am also to do a few dance interludes on the platform. And off we go. Coati drums and I miss my first cue. There is a reprimand for that, and for not getting the melody right, and for not doing the dance steps correctly.

Finally, it comes together. I sing "I – Love – My – Dog" while making circular motions with my paws and hips. Honestly, it's all very embarrassing, but Coati has fun, and that's the point, right? Good, then we can finally trade: the allegedly very rare record for my performance and the warmth and love blanket. I start to doubt this trade though. I simply don't know what this record is worth, so I ask for something else in addition.

Coati doesn't seem to really be surprised, since he already has a plan. He pulls a contract out of his pocket. The contract states that the person who trades for this contract will get 25 percent of the profits of his next single. Considering that Coati Mundi has already been in the top 40 in the US and enjoys a certain amount of fame, it seems like an amazing deal. And Coati actually tells me that songs have already brought him over $100,000. It's crazy—this offer far overshadows the value of the Porsche clock or the three ounces of gold.

Of course there's a catch, as I could have guessed. There are conditions tied to the trade, and they are really something. The single in question will involve my participation: I'll rap in German and Coati will rap in Spanish. Now I understand that the dog song was for more than just Coati's amusement—he wanted to get an idea of my musical talent.

I politely explain that I have never (except for today on the beach) sung before and that I don't have any particular talent in that area. Coati doesn't care. He points to the contract, which says that I have to write at least two rap verses of eight lines each and rap them. I agree, feeling very uneasy. I don't want to be responsible for a good song turning into a total embarrassment.

But that's not all. There is a second condition. In exchange for this trade, he wants something even more embarrassing, right here and now on Venice Beach. He wants to test my acting skills.

I will play Coati's wife's secret lover who was caught in the act and is now feeling the wrath of a betrayed Puerto Rican. And everyone will watch. I really want to have that contract; it could be worth a ton. We hardly have the chance to shake hands and make the deal official when Coati starts to scream at me in Spanish as if he has gone crazy. Once the initial shock wears off, I realize that we are already in the middle of the scene. There's no end to his screaming, and his Spanish curses are really incredible.

"Hombre, muy peligroso, muerto, rapido, la mujer, sexo, sexo, sexo!"

Skateboarders and cyclists stop in shock. A woman fearfully asks me if I need help, but unfortunately I'm not allowed to answer her. I defend myself in German.

"Coati, Coati, es tut mir leid, das mit deiner Frau! Es war keine Absicht, ist einfach so passier und wird nie wieder vorkommen! Bitte alles, nur keine Gewalt!"

But I can't calm Coati's Latin American temper. He pushes me into the baking path, so that everyone has to stop and watch in shock.

He keeps screaming at me in Spanish as if he were being driven crazy with jealousy. And then, completely unexpectedly, he switches to English and yells:

"Five one-handed push-ups, hup hup! Do it!"

Up until this point, I would never have thought that I could do five push-ups on just one hand—but I learned I can. Maybe my fear pushed me to my limits. After the fifth push-up, the passersby start to really worry about me and keep asking if I need help. But then it's all over, the scene is done, and Coati Mundi is the funny little man again, who can hardly keep from laughing. The crowd is totally confused and stares at us in shock. Coati congratulates me, shakes my hand, and hands me the certificate for the 25 percent royalties of the song.

Then it's time to go with Coati to the studio. Cameraman Jakob and I write two verses with sixteen lines each, which Coati later mixes with his own music and lyrics.

Everyone knows—it's the mission of the year,
From nothing to a house, and everyone will cheer.
Number one, I'm in Mainz, an apple I beget,
Number two, apple gone, and I've got some cigarettes.
3, 4, 5, 6, 7, 8, Barterman becomes awake,
9 and 10 to Switzerland, then to India I will take.
One trade after another, it's true the road is long,
Business isn't always easy, and sometimes things go wrong.
Sled, tea, and raw meat, Barterman, what's this crap?
Trade up, and then crash down, some days I want to give up.
With the finest silk in my pack from India to the Land Down Under,
Where the rich man laughs: give the crocs their dinner.
Tanzania, Kenya, oops, I'm in Africa today,
Barterman wants precious stones, but the danger won't go away.
So I'm on the highest mountain, I want to get out of here,
The view is dreamy, and I think of a skyscraper near.

Wake up, let's go, I'm in South America,
No palm trees and no beach but here's a trade Mecca.
So confused, where am I? It's like I'm in Germany,
Lederhosen, folk music, am I in the wrong country?
Car, bird, and anteater, but the last one I can't keep,
Pony, cell phone, porcelain, and Barterman can flee.
Over the big sea. In New York City there's a storm,
The streets are all empty, that makes it hard for barter to take form.
In San Francisco with my costume on the news I take a chance,
Then on CSN I'm immortalized with a crazy chicken dance.
Palm trees, sand, and sun, Coati Mundi invites me,
I meet him at Venice Beach, he wants the trade to be
A rare album, then a contract, but he wants to see me sweat.
I dress up as a dog and sing, then do sit-ups, dance, and beg.
The actor/singer trades with me, it's an experience.
Coati Mundi, Barterman, this song is my big chance.

You can find the video here: www.pichuproductions.de/cme/?page_id=136

Despite my lack of musical knowledge, the song is relatively listenable—at least I think so. However, who knows how much money it will make?

I hardly make it back to my hostel on the edge of LA before the phone rings again. It is Alex Stenzel, who excitedly shares news of another willing trade partner. His buddy Bufo opened the surf shop Hydroflex near San Diego and would love to trade me a surfboard. I can hardly believe my run of good luck, but there is one problem: my flight to Hawaii is in seven hours. To San Diego and back is four to five hours, then there's checking out of the motel, driving to the airport, returning the rental car, and getting all the bartering items onto the plane. That could all take a good ten hours. But a surfboard is the perfect thing for Hawaii. I have to have it! So I take the risk and race to San Diego. I explain my rush to Bufo, and he offers me a new surfboard. I tell him that if possible, I don't want to give up any of the items I have. He understands that, so we make a service trade. I have to clean the surfboard of the famous pro surfer Chris Ward. I hurriedly scrape the wax from the board with my plastic travel insurance card until the card breaks and I'm without travel insurance, physically speaking.

But after ten minutes, the board is clean. Bufo is happy with my work, but he feels like I should give something more. So I go up against his employee Sandy in an arm wrestling match. Sandy is a surfer girl and has upper arm muscles that make mine look like little baby arms. If I win, I can take the surfboard and quickly drive to the airport. If I lose, the board stays with them. Time is running out, so I do what I have to.

Sandy and I kneel in front of the office desk in the surf shop. We tense our arms and look each other deep in the eyes like in the Sylvester Stallone film *Over the Top*, scary and mean through and through. Bufo gives the start signal. We both press as hard as we can. Our faces twist into grimaces, but we don't move one inch. Sandy and I seem to be equal in strength. Even sudden offensives, where we try to force a win with a strong jerk, fail on both sides. After a while, our strength begins to fade, and I am able to push Sandy's arm just a little to the right. That's the deciding moment. I win with the last of my strength. After all that suspense, I jump up cheering and shouting:

"I won! Yeah, I wooon!"

My barter collection for Hawaii is complete:

Three ounces of gold
Valuable Brazilian porcelain
Luxury Porsche clock
Coati Mundi song contract
Photo painting
Two BMX bikes
Record

Surfboard

Overnight coupon for a weekend in LA

A good ten items that now have to be traded for a house with a little piece of land in one of the most heavenly spots on Earth. As happy as I am about this magnificent final stretch, I also know that all of these things do not equal the value of a house.

16

THE SHOWDOWN

Hawaii

The very next morning at seven, I sit with a huge hangover in the studio of the Hawaiian Public Radio. (Dominik and I had to celebrate my spoils in Honolulu—he slept in the bathroom of a YMCA while I knocked indiscriminately on every door in the hostel to find my bed.) Chris Vandercook, the host of the morning show, asks me curiously about the past 180 days.

My head is pounding, and I feel as wobbly in my chair as if we were on a boat in the middle of an ocean during a hurricane. However, I tell him all about it, as much as my condition allows, and want to give out my email after a few minutes. I've hardly had the thought before Chris cuts me off. Public radio in the US does not do advertisements for the interviewee. I'm really annoyed. My compensation is a German song played on the radio: *Mit 66 Jahren* by Udo Jürgens.

Still in my terrible state, I fly from Oahu, the main island with the capitol city of Honolulu, to Big Island, the biggest island in this tropical archipelago. Hawaii is made up of a total of more than a hundred islands, but only a few are inhabited. They are about 2,500 miles from the closest mainland. Despite my hangover, the flight to the big volcanic island revives my childhood dream: sun (average temperature is 88 degrees), beach, waves, rainforest, mountains, palm trees, high waterfalls, and flower-bedecked women. I can hardly believe how beautiful this island really is.

My prospects for trade are much better on Big Island. It is not very heavily populated, so the land prices are much lower than on Oahu or Maui. Additionally, I hear that Big Island is home to many progressively thinking people who use bartering in their everyday lives. Off for the final barter!

Media Offensive, Part Three

Over the last few weeks, I've gathered contacts for Big Island composed of acquaintances, friends of friends, real estate agents, and people who I have met on various online travel and bartering sites.

First I meet Hazen, an expat who I know through Heather, whom I visited once. Hazen had told me previously on the phone that he would speak to various friends who happen to be selling their houses right now. Now he stands on the beach shrugging his shoulders at me, since none of these people answered him.

Then I drive to see Alexander, who lives in the forest with his wife and whom I met through Hazen. He told me in an email that his buddy Lee would like to trade some land. Unfortunately, I have not heard from Lee. Alexander confirms Lee's change of heart and can't help me any further.

Then I go to Jason, who I interviewed two years ago for my project *How to Travel the World for Free*. Jason also lives in the rainforest and gets by completely without money. He hunts wild pigs with his dog and showers in a waterfall. We have been emailing for the past few weeks and he got my mouth watering with a potential land trade, even possibly including a house. But Jason is disappointed with my offerings. He would have loved to fly to Africa with the voucher. He is not interested in objects like bikes, porcelain, or clocks, so he declines to trade.

Then I'm off to see Samantha, who contacted me on Couchsurfing.org about my post seeking a house trade. She wants to split her land and offer half in trade. She's my great hope, but this hope dies when we meet. The housing authority told her that property on Big Island unfortunately can't be split up. We brainstorm for a while, but she doesn't want to get in any trouble, so I have no success there.

The last options on my painstakingly compiled list are various real estate agents who I wrote to about bartering. Almost all of them told me that my chances were good, and three offered to meet me. I visit Jarred, Rose, and Patti, who dig through their lists of clients who would like to barter their house or land instead of selling. But of course, none of the three have any concrete leads.

Disappointedly, I start a new media offensive. We call all available media on Big Island to blare my trade offer over the island. Luckily, Kat from KWXX Radio, the biggest station on the island, gets back to me the next day. I'm invited to the morning show, where the host calls my project "amazing" after an extensive ten-minute interview (this doesn't mean much in America, since everything here is "amazing," even when you just want to say that the food tasted good). However, the two hosts do seem to think my story is pretty good; after the interview, they say my email address six times on the air.

Now I check my emails every minute, but still there's nothing promising. I do get something else though: the biggest daily paper on the island, *Hawaii Tribune Herald*, heard about me on KWXX and wants to interview me right away. Soon, I'm sitting with Colin, a reporter from the paper, who takes a quick picture of me and my offerings after the interview.

I hope that this picture will be in the newspaper in the morning and more people will hear about my mission. But it turns out even better: the headline on the front page is "Barterman Seeks House," with my picture underneath. After a detailed description of my project, they give my email, plain to see for all newspaper readers on the island.

I am almost positive that this report will smooth out the kinks. At the very least, people speak to me on every corner in Hilo, one of two bigger cities on the island.

"Hey Barterman, how's the house?"

"Aren't you Mr. Barterman from the paper?"

"Barterman, help me become an actor!"

I never expected such recognition. Now I'm really confident.

I get my first offer. Eileen, a middle-aged woman, writes that she lives on the northern coast and would like to trade her house. I look at the attached photos that illustrate her offer. I can hardly believe it: it's a huge house right on a beautiful sea cliff with palm trees and a view of the ocean.

Even though it's hard to believe, I jump in my car and visit her. The property is a tropical landscape with an in-ground swimming pool made of volcanic stone with a water slide built in. There's an unbelievable tropical paradise of a garden, a house that could be called lavish, and a view of the sea as promised by the photos. I immediately hold out my hand to shake with Eileen, but she laughs and explains that she is offering a different house on her property. We go up a hill and I see the foundation of a house that is being built. I'm totally disappointed; she really tricked me. I earnestly ask if she's okay in the head. She wants all my items for this foundation. She explains that she saw my story in the media and couldn't believe that Barterman really existed, so she invited me to come to her house; it was a test. She has nothing else to offer.

I look at her quizzically. This is a wealthy, fifty-year-old woman who had me drive two hours across the island just to see if Barterman was real? Eileen apologizes with a laugh, but she can't understand the pressure I've put myself under to trade for a house in the next two weeks. As compensation, I can at least take a dip in her tropical water slide volcano pool so I can be refreshed when I check my email again.

I have just ten days before the two-hundred-day deadline to find the right house and property.

I quickly get to answering the responses that I've gotten through the newspaper. First I meet Tom, who has offered me land. When we meet, he tells me he owns three-quarters of an acre of pretty pastureland, but only wants to trade a thirty-two-square-foot piece. I could hardly put up a tent on that much space.

I drive to meet Clark, another person who heard about me from the newspaper and wants to barter. We meet in a café and he tells me that he owns a big piece of land. But I look at it and see how overgrown it is. It would be impossible to make room for a house in the few days I have left.

Luckily I don't have to debate it for long. I get a message on my cell phone from Jarred, one of the real estate agents. He tells me to come by right away.

He read the newspaper article, too, and was motivated to search for more willing traders. He would love to be the person who brings the bartering blitz to a happy ending. He shows me a quarter-acre piece of land in his files that is in the highland rainforest near Kilauea, a 3,000-foot-high area very appealing to tourists. He says that it only has ferns and a few trees growing on it, so it could be built on right away. I'm totally over the moon and can hardly wait to meet Bill, the owner.

When I meet him on his land, I relax immediately. Bill is seventy-seven, a sort of old hippie, and he greets me with a bottle of tequila. He won't discuss business until both parties have tossed one back. During this nice ritual, he tells me that he thinks my story is great, and even though he is short on money, he wants to be a part of it. I have to keep looking at the land, which looks awesome: 230 feet wide, 500 feet long, level, and with only a few plants. All around there is tall rainforest. In the middle of the land is an old VW bus from the sixties that is crying out to be made into an art object—as a part of my garden. I excitedly show Bill the Porsche clock, an ounce of gold, the Coati Mundi certificate, the overnight coupon from Alex Stenzel, and the Brazilian porcelain. Nothing more, since I still need a house. Bill is excited by the objects and pours me another shot—probably to give himself enough time to think without me chattering on. A moment later, he says that he would like to trade, but that he needs a day to think about it. I agree and have to make it through a long day that feels to me like a week. Bill's offer is a slam dunk!

The next day I call Bill expectantly:

"Hi Bill, have you decided?"

"Not yet, I can't figure out what the Portuguese porcelain is worth."

"It's Brazilian porcelain and is worth about $4,000."

"Okay, but this Coati Mundi certificate is pretty vague."

"Yeah, but I guarantee you I'll have a detailed contract drafted for your 25 percent of the song."

There are more questions about the other items. Once he completely has me sweating in fear that he could pull out, he finally gives me the following answer: "I trust you. It's a deal!"

Crazy! Unbelievable! It's official. I have traded for a 3,200-square-foot piece of land. I'm so excited, but it isn't time to celebrate yet, because I still have to make a house appear somehow.

I go back to my computer and open another email from one of the six real estate agents. It contains the number of an Avery, who apparently builds mobile homes. I can't exactly picture what that would look like, but I drive to visit the man. Avery lives in a tiny house on a huge, black lava field that formed after the eruption of the most active volcano on earth, Kilauea. Avery appears in front of his house in this surreal scenery wearing nothing but shorts; his belly and the big tattoo on his shoulder on display. Because of the risk of tsunamis, his house is built on stilts. There are piles of garbage lying around and it all gives me a funny feeling. I look around, wondering if barking dogs are about to come charging at me. It wouldn't have surprised me, but the situation is just the opposite.

Avery is a very nice person who tells me that he builds homes on trucks to avoid dealing with bothersome building permits. He says that he has a mobile home on offer right now, and he leads me to a little house that could not be any cuter: about eleven feet wide and twenty-eight feet long, completely made of wood, with round portholes, a bedroom, a living room/kitchen, a little bathroom, and a lavish double door, through which you can leave the house and go down a set of retractable wooden steps to the ground.

I feel like it's this house or nothing. I ask Avery if he would like to barter instead of selling. To my great surprise, he agrees immediately and asks what I have to offer. I begin cautiously, with one gold coin. He takes the coin, looks at it, and says that it is not enough. So I add in the art from Alex Stenzel and the record from Coati Mundi. He likes both a lot, but it still isn't enough. So I offer the second gold coin. Now I only have a surfboard up my sleeve. Should I have given Bill less for his land? Avery thinks for a long time, and then asks if I have anything more.

I get the surfboard out of the van, terrified that he's going to want even more, because that would be the end of it! Avery likes it, and he comments that he could easily sell it if he needed money after all. I ask if that's a "yes," and he shakes on it. I could jump for joy! Avery runs off with his loot. I'm ecstatic over this unexpected twist.

In less than two hundred days, I bartered my way from an apple, through fourteen countries, to a house and a piece of property in Hawaii!

It takes hours, even days, until I really feel like I did it. I slowly start to notice the two hundred days of tension and nerves falling away. I sit on the beach on Big Island in the evening and gradually understand that it's over. I did it. Most of all, I achieved my childhood dream.

I HAVE A HOUSE IN HAWAII!

Tonight, Dominik, Jakob, and I really let loose. We've been waiting for this moment for so long. But it's not over yet. One more thing has to be done within the two-hundred-day deadline. I postpone the ultimate celebration a little, so that I remain in working order. I order a flatbed truck to bring the house the twenty-two miles across the island to its future home. Together with its truck, which to my great disappointment no longer works (but you can't have it all), it is hauled across the island.

The drive is not entirely unspectacular. The house on the flatbed blocks two lanes of traffic and has problems with the occasional power line. As we drive the house up the mountain, drivers repeatedly have to pull over so they don't collide with it. The truck driver shows unbelievable talent and patience.

We drive down jungle roads hung with vines, and the creeping plants catch on the roof of the house, which becomes a load test. It keeps creaking and crunching. The ultimate test comes on the property. The house is pulled onto the land by an excavator and it almost tips over sideways. Everyone watching holds their breath. In the last moment, the house threatens to break apart.

But it all works out. The house is parked in the middle of the pasture, and the truck driver surprises me with an unbelievable gift. Instead of taking the agreed-upon $300 for the transport, he just wants the DVD of my bartering blitz TV show in exchange for his work. I'm impressed at how patient and generous he is even after many hours of hard work. I imagine how a house transport like this one would have gone in Germany: to the municipal office, get a permit, handle the paperwork, find a willing truck driver, mark the house with red flags, etc. In this way, at least, Hawaii seems to be a really relaxed and uncomplicated corner of the Earth.

Since I still have the two BMX bikes, I make one last trade with two friends of mine. Their names are Marian Neulant and Axel von Exel. They work as architects, build art pieces, decorate interiors, and create unusual houses. Together, they call themselves Neulantvonexel, NVE for short. They have been excitedly following my whole trip. They immediately say that they will decorate and expand my new house in exchange for the two bikes. With the support of Hazen, Bill, and my new neighbor Bob, we gather enough construction equipment and materials to get started. After a few days, the little house becomes a handsome little farm. The house is newly painted and furnished. There is a little extension with an extra sitting room, new stairs, a little pool by the door, a grill, and many more nice little details to make me feel right at home in the highland rainforest. The light blue house is simply perfect. I can hardly believe that what I am seeing right now all started with one green apple.

Then it's finally time to have a housewarming party in my new barter house. Word has gotten around Big Island that Mr. Barterman actually did it. The party is awesome. Hazen, Heather, Alexander, Bill, the neighbors Rick and Bob, the cameramen Dominik and Jakob, Neulantvonexel, and many new faces from the island pack in. We party like it's going out of style. At the climax of the night, Barterman comes out again in his red superhero costume to enjoy this phenomenal moment with all the guests. It is one of the most fantastic moments of my life. I have fulfilled my long-cherished dream.

EPILOGUE

After two hundred days in fourteen countries and countless highs and lows, the mission is complete. After glorious days with Hermann the riding mower and bad days with the tuk-tuk in India, after terrifying crocodile feedings in Australia, after a hard Kilimanjaro climb in Tanzania, the funny German town in Brazil, the heroic Barterman in New York, the dazzling Burning Man Festival, and the other unforgettable adventures, I reached my goal in the last second. I look back at all the wonderful experiences, adventures, and hardships that all paid off in the end.

In the process, I discovered different bartering cultures: bartering in prison, organized bartering in provincial bartering clubs, bartering as a survival strategy in the slums. I experienced how bartering has a different value from culture to culture. In India, I heard that bartering is totally out and that people are proud of the modern money system, but at the same time, it is obvious that bartering ensures the survival of the poorest of the poor in the slums of Mumbai. I also learned some things about different kinds of exchange, aside from the exchange of goods: successful or failed cultural exchange between countries, the exchange between religions, and the joys and dangers of interpersonal exchange. All these experiences have shown me that all over the world, trade and exchange is so important. People exchange something with every contact, whether it's positive or negative, physical or psychic, abstract or concrete. Exchange seems to be one of the basic aspects of our lives.

It may be that our monetary system functions much more simply than bartering. Not everyone is into carrying their own vegetables to the baker to trade for bread. But there always seems to be situations where people reach back to this ancient form of commerce, whether because the next store is simply too far away, because they have no money, or because there's a war going on. But also often because it is simply more social and much more fun.

Almost all of my transactions excited people; they felt magically drawn to this "old-fashioned" form of commerce. I am still in contact with all of them, including US host Dave Benz, Bill with the property in Hawaii, Peter from Portugal, and Werner in Australia, and I can feel their excitement for bartering. Bartering appears much more sympathetic than monetary commerce, since you have to haggle with your partner for a fair trade much more intensely. At any rate, I have acquired a mountain of new friends and acquaintances because of it.

The most surprising part of my trip is the knowledge of how much you can raise the value of your property with good bartering. From an apple to a house—unbelievable. Of course, you have to be very committed, dedicate yourself completely, and face your fears if you want to convince others to join in with you. But even though I was often plagued by doubts, I never gave up. I stuck to my dream and I made it real.

It would make me happy if my trip (just like in *How to Travel the World for Free*), inspired some of my readers to follow their own dreams. It doesn't have to be a Hawaiian dream house, especially since my travel costs were paid by ZDFneo. Often it is the much simpler things that we dream of our whole lives but never pursue. At any rate, it is a good idea to think about whether our chosen path leaves enough room for our ideas and dreams. Maybe you should take a risk every now and then—just put the pedal to the metal and go!

I stand here with my childhood dream and think that it would be a good idea to share it with others. Until 2015, my house will be open to all who are not scared away by the modest setup, who can accept renting a car to get here, who are happy that it rains in the rainforest, and who don't expect the ocean to be right in front of their nose. You can contact me through my Facebook page, "Michael Wigge – how to travel the world for free."

A joy shared is a joy doubled. So I warmly invite everyone who reads this book to contact me on Facebook under "Michael Wigge" for a visit, because . . .

I am offering:

A one- or two-week stay in Wigge's house in Hawaii

for:

Home improvement

So, if there's a nice little piece of furniture out there looking for a home, or a gifted artist or landscaper who wants to decorate, improve, or expand my house or garden, then she or he should contact me. And if I happen to be enjoying my dream at that moment and am present, I would be happy to have a visit—involving a little test of courage, (for example, jumping over hot lava), or a cool band.

So feel free to write to me. All suggestions are welcome!

Aloha!
Michael Wigge